# Back Roads

## TO THE
## CALIFORNIA COAST

# Back Roads

## TO THE

## CALIFORNIA COAST

*Scenic Byways
and Highways to the Edge
of the Golden State*

EARL THOLLANDER

HERB McGREW

SASQUATCH BOOKS
SEATTLE

Printed in Hong Kong
Distributed by Publishers Group West
09 08 07 06 05 04 03 02        6 5 4 3 2 1

All illustrations and maps: Earl Thollander
Cover design: Michelle Dunn Marsh
Interior design: Karen Schober
Copy editor: Don Graydon

Library of Congress Cataloging in Publication Data

Thollander, Earl.
    Back roads to the California coast : scenic byways and highways to the edge of the Golden State / Earl Thollander, Herb McGrew.
        p. cm.
    Includes index.
    ISBN 1-57061-282-X (alk. paper)
1. California—guidebooks. 2. Automobile travel—California—guidebooks. 3. Scenic byways—California—guidebooks.  I. McGrew, Herb. II. Title.

F859.3 .T48 2002
917.9404'54—dc21                                        2002022385

Sasquatch Books
615 Second Avenue
Seattle, Washington 98104
(206) 467-4300
www.SasquatchBooks.com
books@SasquatchBooks.com

# Contents

7   Dedication

8   Acknowledgments

9   Introduction

1   Salton Sea to the Pacific   15

2   Palmdale to the Sea   29

3   Santa Maria to Santa Barbara   41

4   Santa Maria to the Dunes and Oso Flaco Lake   51

5   Santa Maria to Jalama Beach County Park   59

6   Bakersfield to Morro Bay   67

7   Tulare to Cambria   75

8   King City to Lucia   87

9   King City to Carmel   97

10   Palo Alto to Pescadero   105

11   San Francisco to Point Reyes   113

12   Santa Rosa to the Mouth of the Russian River   121

13   Winters to the Mendocino Coast   133

14   All the Way from Nevada to the Sea   151

15   Eureka to Garberville   161

171   Afterword

173   Index

176   About the Illustrator and the Author

# *Dedication*

*Earl Thollander: 1922–2001*

When Earl and I set off to do the research for this book, the last thing either of us could have imagined was that this would be Earl's last work.

He was full of enthusiasm and happy for another opportunity to meander up, down, and around his native state in search of interesting roads and places and people. But the traveling became increasingly tough: the enthusiasm was there, but the energy was not.

This was unusual, for Earl, though in his late 70s, had rarely been sick and seemed the sort of guy who would go on forever.

His was a household name in the Napa and neighboring valleys: I'm sure more of Earl's paintings and sketches hang in homes hereabouts than do the works of all our other artists combined. He was a fixture, always available to do good work, for which he undercharged, and good works, for which he charged nothing.

When I was growing up, my parents had bad things to say about people with "notions," a difficult-to-define term suggesting affectations or hubris. Earl had fewer notions than anyone I've ever known. Had he won a Pulitzer, he would have said, "Well, that's nice," and gone back to his studio to finish whatever needed to be done. A few days before he died, he said he wanted to be "put in a pine box and buried in my old clothes in the Knights Valley Cemetery." And that's what happened. Keep it simple. And no nonsense.

The best definition I've ever heard of a life properly lived (attributed, curiously, to another artist, James Thurber) was that of "a life lived in accordance with its design." Nobody I've ever known did a better job at that than Earl. His design was not without its idiosyncrasies, but he was true to it from start to finish. That was, perhaps, his greatest art.

# *Acknowledgments*

A number of books were valuable in planning our journeys, especially *Northern California Handbook,* by Kim Weir; *Historical Spots in California,* by Mildred Brooke Hoover, Hero Eugene Rensch, Ethel Grace Rensch, and William N. Abeloe, and revised by Douglas E. Kyle; *The WPA Guide to California* (from Pantheon Books, but originally published in 1939 by Hastings House); *The Smithsonian Guide to Historic America,* text by William Bryant Logan and Susan Ochshorn, editorial director Roger G. Kennedy; and *Glass Giant of Palomar,* by David C. Woodbury. We also made good use of the *San Francisco Chronicle,* the *Los Angeles Times,* the *Michelin Green Guide—California,* and the great maps of the California State Automobile Association.

Many thanks to the geology departments at Humboldt State University and College of the Redwoods for information on the tectonics of the Ferndale region, to B. D. Parmeter for his ornithological assistance, to Dick and Joann Larkey for their wealth of California lore, and to the helpful people at the Lake Berryessa information office.

Thanks also to Jackie Dickson for her Internet assistance; Linda McGrew for her astute, if at times ruthless, editorial advice; Janet Thollander for her delicious meals; and the many pleasant folks we encountered along the way: Caltrans workers at traffic stops, food servers, motel workers, parks people (including Tina of the Dunes), and our fellow travelers.

# *Introduction*

Robert Louis Stevenson, a consummate traveler who spent time in the Napa Valley and Monterey, once noted:

> For travel's sake . . . the great affair is to move; to feel the needs and hitches of our life more nearly; to come down off the feather-bed of civilization, and find the globe granite underfoot and strewn with cutting flints. Alas, as we get up in life, and are more preoccupied with our affairs, even a holiday is a thing that must be worked for.

There's not a lot of cutting flint and granite underfoot these days, but Stevenson had it right. And, if it was true in 1879, what about 2002?

Earl and I love to travel abroad. Who doesn't? But any Californian who focuses on abroad without having seen King's Canyon, or Mono Lake, or the Black Swifts of Burney Falls, or the poppies of the Antelope Valley, or the Carrizo Plain, or Anza Borrego, or Captain Jack's Stronghold, or the otters and whales of Monterey Bay, or . . ., or . . ., or . . . is missing too much too close to home.

The California seen from a road winding through the hills behind Paso Robles or up to Fort Bidwell or over to the Lost Coast is completely different from the California seen by the drivers clenching their teeth along the freeways of Los Angeles and the Bay Area. We all have to cope with traffic on occasion, but doing so demands attending to survival and leaves no time for smelling the flowers.

The idea of traveling and sketching the back roads to the California coast evolved for a number of reasons. Though Earl's been doing "Back Roads" books for thirty years, he's never lost his enthusiasm for another journey. It's impossible to know whether he sketches in order to travel or travels to sketch. Whichever, it's an incurable affliction.

Earl's a visual sort of person and I'm an impressionistic sort. Earl sees things through the eyes of an illustrator (with the great advantage over photographers of being able to leave out the ugly, or to move a pole or a tree). I get impressions. Hence, during our travels, we often reacted differently to what we were seeing. Though the dreary and desolate oil-producing country in the neighborhood of Taft and McKittrick could never be considered "attractive" (and hence was unappealing to ET, a seeker of the picturesque), I, of the East Coast, found it fascinating and functional—worth a detour (well, a short detour). Similarly, I was impressed with the number of truly stark prisons newly scattered about the more desolate regions of the state. Earl was not. *Prisons* did not make the cut.

⌒

Something we're all aware of, but don't think much about, is the extremely mountainous nature of California. The accident of geography that has rather rugged coastal mountains running the length of the state has curbed the building of freeways to connect "coastal" California to "inner" California. Streamside roads winding through forests and canyons are, perforce (and thank goodness), the rule, not the exception as routes to the coast. And not only are the east–west roads through the mountains more picturesque and interesting, there's always that ocean endpoint to each. The idea of having a specific goal, such as a sea or city or mountaintop, makes any journey compelling. (It would certainly be less compelling to do these roads against the grain, eastward *away* from the coast.) There's also that less obvious, more unconscious, and very American (but also universal) longing to be forever heading west.

Aside from telling us our roads should be paved and, barring unusual circumstances, drivable year-round in a two-wheel-drive vehicle, our publisher gave us free rein. Hence, we could follow our whims. We're

sure we "missed" roads that merited inclusion (though not too many: Earl's been a road hawk for fifty years), and some readers will certainly wonder why in heaven's name we included *that* one. No conclusions should be drawn from the choice, for instance, to include (just barely) Carmel but not Monterey, or Santa Barbara but not San Diego. We were arbitrary, avoiding traffic, and trying to be led by the roads themselves. A peculiar mood of a day, an eagle or two, too much traffic, or the serendipitous discovery of a road never driven before might make all the difference. However, we always kept in mind our particular intent to find some routes that would encourage people to head for places they'd never been. Hence, we avoided the likes of Malibu and Yosemite, but included Oso Flaco Lake, Lucia, and the Lost Coast.

It can be a challenge to find a quiet way through the last few miles to the Pacific, particularly down south around, for instance, San Diego and Los Angeles. Not only is the entire coastal region down there being developed in an inland direction, but the state's aforementioned north–south geology has resulted in the aggressive "improvement" of most of the few east–west roads that do exist. Earl had a bad day down there when he found a couple of his old favorites unrecognizable for all their "improvements."

However, if you have a good map and are willing to suffer an occasional false lead or two, a route can usually be devised. On occasion, there might be some bumps and ruts, but those will only assist in keeping the less adventuresome to the freeways.

Here and there you may have to make adjustments in your routes, as Caltrans is forever busy. Earl and I were turned back a couple of times and frequently had to wait when one-lane traffic was the rule. But that was never a problem, and shouldn't be. There's no hurry, and sometimes standing around waiting for the road to open can be quite sociable. I saw my first bald eagle, ever, while waiting at such a stop, and Earl and I had a number of pleasant interludes chatting with

attractive and personable Caltrans women—a phe-
nomenon, unimaginable twenty years ago, that certainly brightened up some of those delays.

Be aware, also, that one of the most exciting—some
would say frightening—aspects of California is its ten-
dency, indeed irrepressible addiction, to be continually
reinventing itself. Things change. Hence, don't be surprised, much less frustrated, if such and such a humble
country restaurant is now a shopping center, or a quiet
country road a superhighway. I'm sure roads and
places changed between our visits and the day this
manuscript was turned over to our editors—and more
have changed since then. If your heart is set on any
particular place, call first and check.

And remember: for whatever their reasons, most
Californians (for that matter, most Americans) are in a
hurry, pathologically so. Most of the roads we've chosen are rural and, though lightly trafficked, will be populated by an inordinate number of pickup trucks and
such. Pull over and let 'em by: they'll love you for it.

⌇

"Land of contrasts." Hopefully, I'll use that faded
phrase only this once. *All* the routes and roads we've
included in this book are rife with contrasts: a green
riparian corridor through an ocean of sand dunes; a
Hearst hacienda that became an officers' club and then
a country inn; a bobcat one minute and a BMW minutes later. That's what makes for interesting journeys.
That's what resulted in this book's being weighted
towards the middle and southern reaches of the state.
This had nothing to do with population density. With
all due respect and even awe vis-à-vis the vast forests
of the north, there *is* a sameness about them. (Seen
one mountain, seen 'em all?)

And I've always overused the expression "the middle of nowhere." But these are the places Earl and I
fancy—and "in the middle of nowhere" is itself an
evocative term. It can be just as awesome watching a
sunstruck yellow-headed blackbird on the open range as
spotting an eagle in the mountains. A single wildflower

pushing through the alkali dust of the vast Carrizo Plain
can be more stirring than myriad poppies. Maybe that's
because such austere sightings require more of "us."
One can *oooh* and *aaah* at an eagle, but that's mostly
because of the eagle. Appreciating the triumph of that
flower's survival is a different kind of experience.

I've also been accused of chronic hyperbole. There
are worse crimes. Hyperbole is, however, difficult to
avoid in bigger-and-better-than-anywhere-else
California.

California has its share of environmental problems,
but because of its diversity and pioneering environmental attitudes, it's a wonderland of wildflowers and
whales and birds. As all our routes course through
attractive open country and/or forests, and finish by
the sea, all can be good—or great—venues, depending upon the season, for wildflowers, whale-watching,
and birding. This is sort of a given, so I haven't continually noted it. The wildflowers are particularly profuse
in the spring, but there are *always* flowers if you really
look. Though most of California's "coastal whales" are
seasonally migrating grays, there are always whales or
porpoises or other creatures out there—not in profu-
sion, perhaps, but unless you really look, you'll never
know. And of course, there are birds of every sort,
many of which do not require a degree in ornithology
to identify. A pileated woodpecker can brighten up the
grayest of days; a chattering kingfisher can warm the
heart of almost anyone.

I *have* noted some of the birds we saw, one reason
being that I'm much better with the birds than the
flowers, which, it seems to me, have names requiring a
working knowledge of Latin to identify. If the least bit
interested in these items, make sure you bring a
(good) bird and/or wildflower book. (There are endless, often contentious, debates in the birding community as to what is a "good," much less "the best," bird
book: Peterson's venerable *Field Guide to Western Birds?*
The new *Kaufman?* The old *Robbins?* The *National
Geographic Field Guide to the Birds of North America,* or

the fat new *Sibley Guide to Birds?* For non-crazed bird-ers, I think Peterson is the best. There being far more flowers than birds, flower-watchers have a more diffi-cult time: again I think the Peterson Field Guide Series *A Field Guide to Pacific States Wildflowers* is best.)

We did the best we could to scatter our choices up and down the coast, with some short routes and some of greater length. Length is, obviously, arbitrary: a route can be picked up anywhere along the way. We start one route (Chapter 14) at the Nevada border—for a fleeting moment we considered running all our routes clear across the state, but that's for some other time. The chapters are arranged in the order we did them, from south to north, but can be done any which way. Some, of course, are likely to be done in conjunc-tion with each other: Santa Maria to Santa Barbara, the Dunes and Jalama Beach County Park, for instance, or King City to Lucia and Carmel.

We've handled distances in various ways. Earl's maps have the significant mileages, as will your road maps; sometimes I note mileages in the text, sometimes not. It gets tiresome, and I figure no two cars count the miles exactly alike. And anyway, if you're traveling at a proper pace, so what if you miss a turn or two? You might come up with something better than we did.

And along the same line, the time one spends on any of our routes can vary to the Nth power, so the suggested times in the chapter headings are merely guesses. If you're into flower-watching and/or birding and/or photography and/or picnicking, you could spend much more time; if you're into testing out your new Porsche, hours could become minutes.

⌣

What to bring? If you're the sort of traveler we are, or recommend you should be, you can never have too many maps. Mostly we used AAA maps. Disregarding the other services they offer, AAA maps are worth the price of membership.

We used a California map, regional maps, county maps, city maps—and two different California road atlases, the Thomas Brothers *California Road Atlas & Drivers Guide* and the Benchmark Maps *California Road & Recreation Atlas.* Our conclusion: no map has *every-thing.* Indeed, it sometimes seems the specific item you're after has been intentionally left off the map you have in hand. Look for missions and you'll find reservoirs. Look for wineries and there are missions everywhere. Look for a park and all you can find are wineries.

You should also have motel and hotel listings. Chambers of commerce and tourist bureaus are excellent sources, as are the AAA guides. Earl and I don't like to book ahead, for we're never quite sure where we might finish a day; some people aren't com-fortable with that. That's a matter of choice.

I also think a decent pair of binoculars is an *essential* for any traveler, regardless of whether or not one is into birding or star-watching or whatever. For one thing, binoculars are often the item that *converts* non-birders into birders and/or watchers of other things. And, if you believe the statistics, birding—a nontoxic, wildlife-preserving, inexpensive, socially pleasant, and undemanding sport that can be practiced by anyone, in the middle of a metropolis or a desert—is the most popular spectator sport in the nation.

Binoculars are handy in other ways: moon- and planet-watching, checking out distant road signs, crea-ture-watching, and, if you look through them upside down, they double as an excellent magnifying lens for examining tiny bugs or the inside of flowers.

There are chambers of commerce in most towns and they're becoming increasingly sophisticated in their ability to assist travelers and visitors. With people far more interested in eating well, tourist bureaus and C of Cs are keeping current on their local restaurants and wineries. In the past, wildlife-watchers were con-sidered penny-pinching oddballs, but there's now, for instance, a motel in Fort Bragg that provides, in every room, a list of local restaurants *and* a brochure describing the birds to be seen from the back balcony!

⌣

While Earl and I are in many ways dissimilar, there's one common ground that makes light of other issues: food. No matter how any day has gone, we always look forward to the evening's quest for a decent meal.

I've always had my own, I suspect unconscious, reactions to restaurants. The older I've become, the more these reactions are based on such matters as ambiance and attitude (and, I must admit, wine prices) than on the main course items. I've found wonderful places in the boonies I wouldn't go near at home and wonderful places at home I wouldn't go near in the boonies.

If a good meal is as important to you as to Earl and me, bring anything that could help in the restaurant department: newspaper clippings, *Zagat* and/or other restaurant guides, and the stuff from the local chambers of commerce and tourist bureaus.

*Or*, rely on your intuition. Whenever I travel, with Earl and/or others, there are sundry duties to be spread amongst the group: route-finding, map-reading, motel-finding, weather-watching, and so forth. My assignment is that of restaurant-finding. While I have been known to rely on all of the above printed materials, I rely mostly on my incredibly sophisticated intuitive capacity to pick up on the sort of vibrations that emanate from both the best and worst of eating places. The downside of this remarkable gift is that even the most gifted of intuitives are probably right no more than 71 percent of the time. Hence, while often a hero in my capacity to choose *the* jewel from amongst a selection of restaurants, I often make colossal errors—which my companions, expecting perfection, remember far longer than my triumphs.

Earl and I had *remarkable* luck with our meals while researching this book. In fact, we had so many good breakfasts, lunches, and dinners that we eventually decided it wasn't luck at all, but the changing nature of "eating out" in the USA. Restaurants are paying attention, to their food and the quality of their help. Hooray! We were rarely disappointed, whether it was

ridiculously cheap Mexican-American, Danish modern, sushi, fast food, quaint "European," traditional American, crack-of-dawn casino, Italian, shopping-center Chinese, or some unusual combinations of the same.

My standard benchmark lunch is the classic American BLT. In the course of our travels, not only did Earl and I never have a BLT we didn't like, we had some of the best ever—one of which registered 3.92 out of a possible 4 stars!

Few of our meals were extraordinary in the pure culinary sense, but considering where we were eating them and what we were paying, many were extraordinary. And when you're on the road—at least when Earl and I are on the road—a laidback meal that includes a fresh green salad (a year-round California perk), some crusty bread, and a draft bottle of beer or bottle of decent wine is three quarters of the way home. You don't need the the Ritz in Indio.

⌣

Before setting off on the touring necessary to put this book together, I had never traveled California with a diligent eye. I was always on some sort of a holiday lark. Traveling with Earl, however, was an education, and it changed the way I look at things—probably forever. As a rule, I'd been a lazy traveler, apt to muse while driving along, thinking more about my next meal than the encircling landscape. However, when you think you might be retelling the trip to a stranger or reporting on it (particularly if you've been paid an advance with the understanding that you're going to report it with brilliance and wit), your eye sharpens: you see more and you see it differently. *It* becomes more important than one's musings.

Hence, I would recommend that whenever any of us travel, for whatever reason, we assume we're on duty. At the least, tell that inner eye to *pay attention*.

*Chapter One*

⌇

SALTON SEA
TO THE PACIFIC

*Through desert
and mountains to a
classic Southern California
meeting with the sea.*

*If Palomar is included,
156 miles—a long day.*

*These are the Borrego Badlands with the Santa Rosa Mountains
as a backdrop. I sketched the red-shouldered hawk with its
captive snake at the Anza-Borrego visitors center
in Borrego Springs, adding it to
this drawing.*

# SALTON SEA TO THE PACIFIC

While there's plenty enough variety in California to provide a lifetime of intriguing traveling, there's nothing quite so unique as the extreme southern reaches of the state. Hence, it seemed appropriate for our first undertaking that Earl and I go about as far as we could in California, and start in the desert.

We didn't want to get too close to the overdone Palm Springs scene, so we spent the night in Indio, just north of the Salton Sea.

Now, I'm a relatively seasoned traveler, but the first time I passed through these parts, chasing birds in the early '70s, I couldn't believe I was still in the USA. With its sand and sun and palms, it looked more like something out of the *Arabian Nights.* So before Earl and I got down to work, I thought we should look around to see if much had changed since then.

Well, Indio's still the date capital of the western hemisphere: National Date Festival, date shakes, date ice cream. And nearby, Thermal's still thermal, appropriately named, as it's often the hottest spot in America—and occasionally the world.

The Salton Sea is a most remarkable place. A gigantic lake formed by the overflow from a flooding Colorado River in 1905, it's unlike any other sea in America. Lying well below sea level, with no outlet, and precious little inflow, it's a huge endangered puddle, most similar perhaps to the Dead Sea, the lowest place on earth. It's no Tahoe, but it sure is interesting—to fishermen, birders, and anyone interested in agriculture. The acreage surrounding the lake is some of the most productive, visually compelling, and unusual farmland to be found anywhere: midst the sand, a mix of brilliant green citrus, row crops, vineyards and, of course, date palms.

There are palm trees all over California, but none like these. These are serious, *working* palms, not wimpy ornaments. Often their bunches of maturing dates are bagged or sacked while still on the tree to protect them from the weather and the sundry critters who might harvest them prematurely. Many of the trees are huge, with ladders attached up high to aid during harvest.

The climate, sunny and dry and often extremely hot, can be daunting in summer—which is why the Salton Sea is not on the main line for visiting—but it's delightful in winter. To prove, however, that this region *can* be visited at any time of year, Earl and I chose what would probably be considered an almost suicidal moment to go, during a July heat wave.

We took off from Salton City, halfway down the west shore of the lake, on Route S22. It was early and we were coffee-charged and ready to go. We had gone only a mile or two, toward Anza-Borrego Desert State Park, when we came upon a scene so appealing that it was hard to believe it wasn't a setup. There, atop a

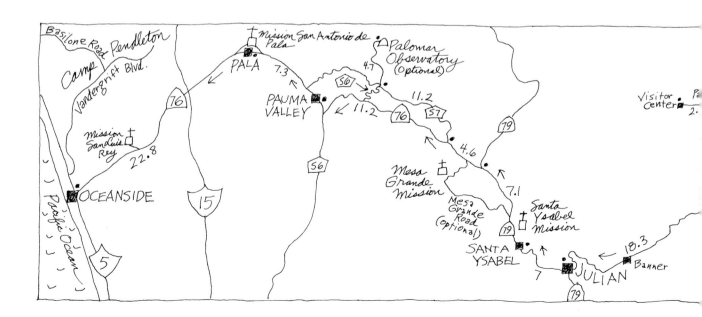

dune, was a little old man sitting on a camp stool in the brilliant morning sun, waving to us—and pointing to his sign held high: Love Peace. We couldn't think of a better send-off, and hoped—indeed, presumed—this

to be the best of omens, for this trip and those to come.

After a few miles we were into Anza-Borrego park. I'd heard of Anza-Borrego, but having fallen in love with the deserts of New Mexico and Arizona as a youth—and having been less than impressed with what I thought was *the* California desert, the Mojave—I wasn't expecting much. I was mistaken. Even in July, Anza-Borrego is spectacular. Its subtle colors and varied plant life—always surprising in such unforgiving habitat—merit a special journey.

It's thirty miles on Route S22 from Salton City to Borrego Springs, the full-service town surrounded by the park. We took our time. The light was right and even on this, one of the major roads in the park, there was nobody around. A few miles into the park, we stopped to take in the vast landscape leading across to the Santa Rosa Mountains and experienced something rare these days: the first car that came along stopped and asked if we were OK. That this happened again on other country roads was more than reassuring, and had us feeling better about having left the cell phones at home.

We drove through Borrego Springs and on to the somewhat cavelike park visitor center just west of town. It's in a beautiful spot, with trails and good signage describing what was spread out before us: the trees, the cacti, the San Ysidro and Santa Rosa Mountains, the Borrego Badlands, Borrego Sink, and even a place called Alcoholic Pass.

At first it seemed there was no life about, but as usual, patient watching confirmed the oft-noted observation that there's *always* life, even in the harshest of circumstances. Bees and bugs and dragonflies appeared. Here and there some tiny verdins, classic birds of the desert, worked the creosote bushes. Pupfish swam in the pond, and an occasional chipmunk

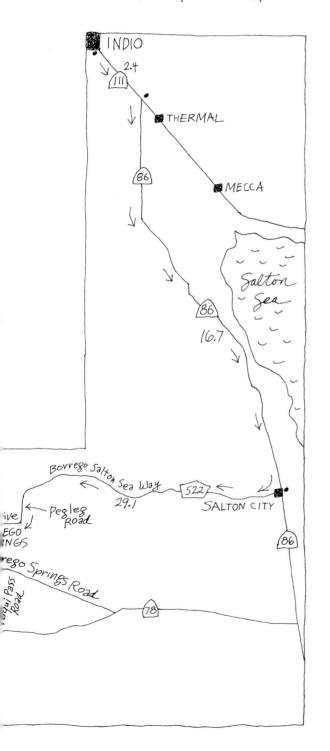

inched in for a drink. There was even a bicyclist, once from Borrego Springs but now living in "It's cold all the time" San Diego—so cold that every once in a while he has to come back to the desert for "a heat fix."

The headquarters staff were pleasant and informative, so we hung around for a while, but when we decided to leave they got serious. It was warming up outside, with a predicted high of 107 degrees. (No big deal. It had hit 124 a few days before: *that's* thermal!) As we went out the door, we were cautioned to drink plenty of water and were handed a brochure titled "Don't Die in the Desert!!" That caught our attention. But they weren't really as concerned with such as we, who were sticking to the main roads, as with the true desert rats bold enough to head into the backcountry.

*Trees all but obscure this historic building in Julian. I moved branches to show more architecture. The former Santa Ysabel School was moved to this location and restored in 1971 as a San Diego County library.*

Anza-Borrego merits more time than we gave it. I'd like to return when the park's famed wildflowers are in bloom. Marginally tolerable in July, the park is delightful in the fall, winter, and spring. We could, however, appreciate the comments of one less-than-impressed nineteenth-century pioneer who passed through these parts on a wagon, calling the place "an inhospitable cheerless sand ravine and mountain waste, but such is the overland trip to California." Count your (air-conditioned) blessings.

We left town to the south on Route S3 and after a dozen miles turned to the west on Route 78. We originally thought we'd stay with 78 all the way to the sea, but we meandered, figuring that as long as we were heading in a generally western direction, meandering was OK.

As Route 78 climbed into the hills west of the park, the temperature moderated and, after the road went up and over a couple of ridges, the scene changed. The sands of the desert gave way to green-brown scrub and then, rather suddenly, changed again. As we descended steeply into Banner, we came to an inland island of lush forest that, we suspected, the populace of this tiny settlement consider their private Shangri-la. The desert was forgotten.

After bottoming out down there, we started our first serious climb, which brought us up to 4,220 feet and our next destination, Julian. A charming, late nineteenth-century mountain town that had a gold rush starting in 1869, Julian's eventual destiny was not to be in gold, but in tourists.

Luckily for Earl and me, that's rarely a problem. Tourists *can* be irritating, but so can politicians, car salesmen, telemarketers, in-laws, and myriad others— and, in truth, most American tourists are OK. As I said, they don't bother Earl and me. When Earl goes into his

sketching (dare I say right-brained) mode, he's in a zone. You could surround him with the Balkans and he wouldn't notice. And I'm a people-watcher, someone who doesn't mind, for instance, sitting for hours in airports watching the passing parade.

However one feels about the visitors, Julian's a pleasant place, with a great climate, some interesting old buildings, and an intriguing history. How could you not love a town where you can buy homemade chocolate in a house built by one Almon Phineas Frary Jr. in 1897?

To those of us who travel on our stomachs, tourism everywhere has resulted in an extraordinary increase in the opportunities to eat well. While Earl was sketching Julian's old library, I initiated my usual routine: in the country, grab the binoculars, go for a walk, and do some birding; in town, a walkabout, some people-watching, and then my most important responsibility, finding a proper place to eat. Julian has the full spectrum in that department, something for everyone. I noticed the pie signs first; indeed, a couple of places specializing in nothing *but* pies—and a reactionary restaurant with a sign that promised all sorts of choices, "But No Pies." This finally made sense when we learned that after Julian's gold ran out, apples were in.

At the west end of the main street, past most of the action, I found just what we wanted, the Julian Grille, a quiet place serving good food, beer, and wine, out on a thoroughly shaded patio. I retrieved Earl and brought him back for just the sort of lunch we hoped we'd enjoy on our first day out. It was a most successful interlude, enhanced by some fine local wine, a good example of the ever-increasing numbers of well-made wines from places we wine snobs of the Napa Valley have never heard of.

Just outside Julian, Route 78 merges with 79. We continued for seven miles to the intersection where the

two roads go their separate ways. Route 78 does continue on to the sea at Oceanside, but we think the
northerly 79 is more interesting. After another
seven miles, through classic California meadows
and woodlands, we turned to the northwest onto
Route 76. The considerable hills of the Cleveland
National Forest are off in the distance, and atop the
tallest is an imposing white tower, the now venerable
Palomar Observatory.

On our routes we try to avoid side trips, but
Palomar is worth the time and effort. The fabrication
of Palomar's giant two-hundred-inch glass reflecting
mirror, still the largest of its kind, caught the nation's
interest during the difficult 1930s and '40s. It was to be
a great leap forward, the ultimate instrument that was
going to reveal the secrets of the universe. And it did,
at least *some* of the secrets, with its pioneering
research into such as the physical constitution of
stars and the nature of supernovas and the
expanding universe. Those who imagined, and
then built, Palomar thought that "it may
never be possible to look farther afield
than with this," but they had not imagined journeys to the moon, or the
Hubble Space Telescope.

A visit to the observatory
adds some driving time off
Route 76, but the roads
up and down (Route
S6 from the west, S7
from the east), with
their excellent sur-
face, sweeping curves,
and great views, are
themselves worth the
diversion.

*Mission San Antonio de Pala is on the Pala Indian
Reservation. I sit in deep shade drawing and listening to the
banter of Indian boys joking and laughing across the road.*

*A great blue heron walking about with a wriggling fish in its beak. It is early morning. There are many visual treats to the eye, with the vacation folk, sky-high palms, sea birds, boats, and a lighthouse added just for picture interest.*

The observatory, still active and contributing, welcomes visitors and should be visited. It is *extremely* impressive. Indeed, its cool, dark, and soaring interior is cathedral-like, almost mystically so.

At the bottom of the mountain, the route continues on into Pauma Valley: nurseries everywhere, citrus groves bordered by the lushest oleanders we'd ever seen, and the first of a number of sites where the challenge seemed to be that of growing avocados on slopes as near vertical as possible. About seven miles past Pauma Valley, still on 76, we arrived at the principal reason for selecting this route, Mission San Antonio de Pala.

The twenty-one California missions were established in the nineteenth century by the Spanish padres for the purpose of spreading the gospel amongst the native population of southern and central California. As is the case with so many well-meaning endeavors, there were positive and negative aspects of the mission experience. One must, however, give the padres credit for their admirable architectural sensibility and their introduction of some Old World agricultural products—wine grapes and olives in particular—that have become California staples.

Earl and I weren't planning to pay particular attention to the missions but, for a number of reasons, we eventually spent considerable time, and ink, on the ones we visited. With their architectural honesty—so contaminated by their modern interpreters—and genuine vestiges of spirituality so lost in the shuffle of our crazed modern lives, they are an invaluable something in the midst of so much spiritual nothingness.

Earl, a California native drawn to the visual beauty of the missions and the sort of backcountry places where many of them were established, knew more about the missions than I, but we agreed in the course of our travels that the two San Antonios, de Pala and de Padua (Chapter 8), were the most impressive.

Officially founded in 1816, San Antonio de Pala has had a tough time of it, its survival endangered by earthquakes, floods, and the politics and secularization of its early years. But with numerous minor, major, and often just-in-the-nick-of-time restorations, it survives, architecturally and spiritually—and is the only mission still serving the Native American population.

The interior of de Pala's sanctuary comes closest, we think, to what the mission experience was—and is—all about. Though dark and horizontal below its massive beams, the wall paintings and ambience of the place render it bright with color and spirit.

Contiguous with the Pala Indian Reservation, the mission is surrounded by outbuildings: a campanile, unique in that it stands away from the sanctuary; a school; and a cemetery, which affords a particularly poignant history of the place. There are simple wooden crosses scattered about on the grounds; new graves and old, of Latinos, Native Americans, Anglos—and those of a number of children, with their toys and dolls and favorite candies piled about their crosses.

Route 76 from San Antonio de Pala to the coast gets busy now, but it's interesting: nurseries, orchards, some vast tomato fields and, eventually, the smell of the sea.

And then our first arrival on the coast. It was obvious as we drove into town that Oceanside was, on this summer Sunday afternoon, one lively spot. Some of the city seemed newly done, while some had an older art deco look to it. There were crowds of young and beautiful Californians enjoying the scene, and each other. It was all very upbeat, except that Earl and I clearly were the oldest people in the world—an impression oft-repeated in the course of our travels.

There was certainly enough action to keep us busy

for a while. I did the town. Earl did the beach, which was the real thing, with colorful umbrellas, splashing kids, and lifeguard towers with bona fide lifeguards—something one never sees up north, where only the rubber-clad and foolish go into the "other," cold Pacific.

Later, after settling into a motel, we set off to the north end of town and Oceanside Harbor, to choose from a collection of indoor-outdoor waterside restaurants a place to celebrate our successful day. We had carelessly forgotten, however, that it was high dining hour. There wasn't a parking place to be had, and the whole harbor appeared to be overbooked. So, after escaping to a quiet side street, we looked over the list of restaurants noted by the tourist bureau and chose a Thai place at the south end of town. Upon entering, however, we both decided it was rather grungy and a bit too down-home—even for us. Back to the drawing board.

Just a short walk up the street was "A Taste of Europe," so we decided, with some trepidation, to try it—and proceeded to have a most delightful evening. Open only a few years, and maybe a bit retro for Oceanside, the place is a kick, and *is* a taste of Europe—not current Europe, but the sort of old-fashioned, decorated-to-its-hodgepodge-teeth restaurant that one finds in the old towns of middle Europe, where the tenth generation of a family is hanging in there, sticking to the old ways. It was like a set from an old Hungarian movie, and we couldn't tell if they really thought that's what restaurants are looking like these days or if they *wanted* it to look that way.

After towering napkins were plucked from giant wine goblets and laid on our laps, we were treated to a good meal, a bottle of fine 1998 Côtes du Rhone, and some moments as far from the world of Oceanside as could be imagined.

Early the next morning, we returned to the harbor, now as quietly peaceful as it had been frenetic the night before. Earl had the nearly deserted scene to himself. The only folks about were boat people, out for their morning constitutionals. For the next hour, I walked and watched. The vast marina—which advertises itself as the friendliest in the territory—is quite an operation. It must also be one of the busiest, for every one of its nearly one thousand slips was taken. Hence, while Earl worked, there was plenty for me to see, including haggling pelicans and dainty egrets on the south side and a heronry high in a eucalyptus to the north.

## ANOTHER ROUTE TO TRY

If possible, do some exploring before setting off on this trip. What first meets the eye appears too hot and harsh to be of much interest, but if, for instance, you drive around the east side of the Salton Sea on Route 111, you will wind up with a better picture of the strange diversity of this region. If you're into birding, stop at the refuges at the north end and along the east shore—good places for unusual sightings. There was even a Laysan albatross that hung around for a while a few years back.

Calipatria, down near the southeast end of the Salton Sea, has the distinction of owning the tallest flagpole in the nation. With Calipatria at 187 feet below sea level, the city fathers long ago decided, appropriately, that it would be insulting to Old Glory to fly her that low. Hence, the flagpole. For miles around it's the only item operating in the black.

And off in the distance to the east of the Salton Sea is the most intriguing scene of all, the Chocolate Mountains. Who would not want to spend some time *there,* on a hot day, with the mountains oozing lusciousness? But alas, it would appear that we are unwelcome. On the map: "No Travel, Closed to the Public, Impact Area." Impact of what? From where? By whom? Travelers from Area 51? On another map: "Chocolate Mountain Naval Reservation Aerial Gunnery Range." Enough said.

## SOME PLACES WE LIKE

✘ Anza-Borrego Desert State Park; (760) 767-5311.

✘ Julian Grille; 2224 Main Street, Julian; (760) 765-0173.

✘ Palomar Observatory; (760) 742-2119.

✘ A Taste of Europe; 1733 South Coast Highway, Oceanside; (760) 722-7006.

*Chapter Two*

PALMDALE TO THE SEA

*A mountainous
run to the north of
Los Angeles.*

*A journey of 155
miles—a half to a
whole day.*

*It is a calm, quiet day in San Juan
Capistrano. Just sitting, drawing
the mission, serenely white,
promotes that same
feeling within me.*

# PALMDALE TO THE SEA

Palmdale isn't particularly convenient to anywhere. It is, however, an appropriate place to start this route. Get there as you will and spend the night.

Except for a pleasant hour at the mission in San Juan Capistrano, a visit to the Tucker Wildlife Sanctuary north of there, and a sushi stop, getting to Palmdale consisted of a tedious circumnavigation of Los Angeles. We arrived there tired, hot, and hungry.

Palmdale is in the midst of a transformation—typical these days—from old California to new, which in a number of ways favors the traveler. There is, for instance, a full range of motel offerings. As is our routine, we

drove through the parking lots of a couple of cheap places, trying to intuit from these thirty-second inspections the sort of situation we're always looking for: no frills, clean and quiet.

Many of the original budget Motel 6s, 8s, and such could be pretty grim. I gave up on them years ago, but Earl and I stayed at some that were more than adequate. We also stayed at a couple that weren't, but that's another story—titled, perhaps, "Intuition, the Imperfect Science." But even when they're not so hot,

it's no big deal. Hotels and motels are only for sleeping. Why spend money for a bed when you can spend it on food and drink?

That, of course, was our next challenge. When there's no time for a meandering perusal of the local restaurants, one has to resort to other approaches: newspapers and/or the Yellow Pages and/or in-depth interviews with the locals. This last can be challenging, but also fun. Obviously you do not seek advice at the desk of a motel that has its own restaurant, and as a rule, not from teenybopper desk clerks or, God forbid, gas station attendants. On occasion, when searching for a good meal, I'll call a wine shop. They'll know. I've even walked into hospitals and asked the nurses.

Tourist bureaus are tricky, as they're not supposed to favor particular eateries, but sometimes you can approach them with something like: "I looked in the Yellow Pages and saw an ad for such and such a restaurant. Would I be making a big mistake if I went there for dinner?" Or, "I'll name three restaurants on the list you gave me. If you were going out to eat tonight, which would you choose?" Etc.

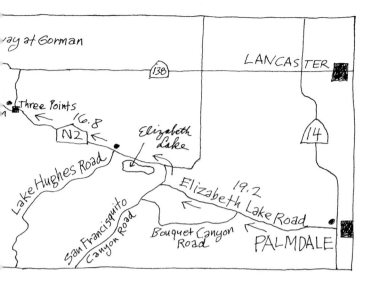

On this particular night, however, we had to get on with it; no time for sophisticated research. We approached the teenyboppers at the desk. As it was hot and we were thirsty, Mexican food and beer was the logical choice.

We asked. They answered, of course, that "El Toreo, just down the road, serves fab Mexican food."

And it does! Nice place, nice people, and a choice of buffet or table service. We chose the former and could have done ourselves in on good Mexican food for $6.95 a head (not including the beer). For those used to paying $6.95 for three beets and a crouton, amazing. We drove back to the motel, thanked the young women at the desk (no longer teenyboppers) for their astute recommendation, and retired.

*It is a very hot day as the birds enjoy the feeders at the Tucker Wildlife*
*Sanctuary, which we visited en route to Palmdale. No hummingbirds have arrived.*
*The attendant in the shop here remembered me from my visit thirty years ago.*

*Joshua trees, with their hairy coats, are much in evidence around Palmdale.*

In the morning it became clear that while I'd been dodging SUVs en route to Palmdale, Earl had been diligently laying out this day's route. After a couple of cups of Styrofoam coffee and some sweet rolls, we set off directly west on Elizabeth Lake Road (Route N2). As is typical of so many booming cities such as Palmdale, the transition from populated to deserted can occur rather suddenly: new roads, new houses, and new Jack-in-the-Boxes one moment, old ranches, horses, and Joshua trees the next.

Elizabeth Lake Road becomes that Western very quickly and follows the ever-lurking San Andreas Fault, which explains why it's so straight in such hilly, crooked country. The hills on the left soon become mountains, and the Antelope Valley is over the ridge to the right.

After fifteen miles, with the road gaining altitude along the way, you pass some homes and activity along the edge of Elizabeth Lake and Hughes Lake, a quiet scene only minutes out of Palmdale but far removed in

ambience. If it's spring or early summer and you're game for a short detour, the Antelope Valley California Poppy State Reserve is only a few miles from Elizabeth Lake. There's a signed right turn at the lake. It's good to call ahead to check on the status of the wildflowers, as the timing of the display varies from year to year.

Fifteen miles or so past the lakes, and still climbing, you come to the piney woods settlement of Three Points, so named because the only three roads in the territory merge here. Three Points is *truly* an outpost, and if you stand in the intersection (no need to worry about traffic), it's just not possible to envision that you're in Los Angeles County. I'm sure that many of the folks who live in this and other such high-country outbacks have never been over the mountains to Tinseltown and are ill at ease with being in the same county as that scene. Indeed, off and on over the years, a number of north-county communities have tried to garner support for secession, but so far no luck.

Three Points has only one (seldom open) commercial establishment, the funky old Three Points Historic Roadhouse Bar & Grill—Earl's kind of subject. While he worked, I walked and did some serious birding. For whatever reason, there were birds everywhere. In addition to the usuals, there were Bullock's orioles, Western kingbirds (preoccupied with harassing the local common ravens), and a remarkable number of phainopeplas, never an everyday bird anywhere.

Elizabeth Lake Road terminates in Three Points, but Pine Canyon Road continues directly on for about ten miles, still along the fault. Far more birds, rabbits, and wonderful old oaks than traffic. We turned right onto Ridge Route Road and descended to its intersection with Route 138. Then it was 138 past rather sterile Quail Lake, and a right onto Gorman Post Road, which in turn leads under Interstate 5 and into Gorman.

You will now have the pleasure of encountering the steep Grapevine grade of Interstate 5 without having to suffer it. Gorman's function is to service this famed highway climb into the wilds of Los Angeles County, and it's eternally busy doing so, what with boilings-over in the summer and all manner of problems experienced by the multitudes of winter drivers who cannot bring themselves to acknowledge that snow and ice *can* occur so close to La La Land.

We slipped down along the west side of the Grapevine on Peace Valley Road to Frazier Park Road and turned into the town of Frazier Park. Here's the place to make sure you have plenty of gas, because there's nothing but wilderness for the next couple of hours.

Three miles west of Frazier Park we turned onto Lockwood Valley Road and into the genuine wilds of Los Padres National Forest. It's very impressive country. It's also condor country.

In the old days, before the last of the wild condors were trapped for the captive breeding program, the best place to see condors was from atop Mount Pinos, at 8,831 feet the highest peak in the region. It's just to

*At the intersection of the Three Points, Pine Canyon, and Elizabeth Lake Roads is this structure of some antiquity. Although gas and groceries are no longer sold here, on occasion it still functions under the elongated title "Three Points Historic Roadhouse Bar & Grill."*

*There is a pink pig mailbox along
Lockwood Valley Road.*

the north of Lockwood Valley. The idea was to scan the skies to the southeast, toward the Sespe Condor Sanctuary, searching for these great soaring birds. Once, in 1972, I spent hours up there on a scorching day gazing off in that direction and saw nothing until someone suggested that the birds were not to the south but to the north, where they rode the thermals above the San Joaquin Valley. I finally did see a few, but they could just as well have been airplanes, as distant as they were. A couple of years later, as I was cranking up the Grapevine and ruminating about that less-than-satisfactory experience, I almost ran down a swooping condor, larger than life.

So it's worth stopping at the pull-outs and vista points along Lockwood Valley Road to check out the vast spectacle surrounding you. Scanning for condors gave me something to do while Earl sketched, and I spent an hour or so at that, hoping for the best. Earl has never seen a condor, so it's too bad that none appeared—but uncertainty is what birding's all about.

After about twenty-seven miles, Lockwood Valley Road terminates at Route 33, where we turned south and headed for Ojai. After some curvy climbing up to Pine Mountain Summit (at 5,080 feet), 33 descends into the Sespe Gorge. During my condor-chasing trips, I had traveled near here, but never down into the gorge itself. It's a dramatic ride on a good road—not to be missed.

Even in late July there was plenty of water in Sespe Creek, so the gorge was green with cottonwoods and undergrowth; hummingbirds along the creek, red-tailed hawks up above. Not only is it a much better than average gorge (anywhere else in the world it would be a national park), but it's also educational. At perhaps the gorge's most gorgeous point a whole mountainside has been knocked askew, almost to vertical, to form a side of the creek bed, a most impressive demonstration of the cantankerous nature of the earthquake faults that trouble the region. And everywhere, intriguing clues—water stains, logjams, and deep gulches—as to what it must be like when the rains do come, as they tend to do, with a vengeance.

Route 33 continues, next through Wheeler Gorge, and on into the environs of Ojai.

When I first visited Ojai, some thirty years ago, it had seemed the epitome of what California was all about. I'd seen beaches and oceans and mountains and canyons and all that, but never the combinations of golden fields, open oak woodland, and quiet mission-style architecture that abounded in this then small town. There was an aura about it, the same sort of undefinable something that one experiences in Provence or Santa Fe or, curiously (though very much of a different nature), mid-Manhattan; manifestations of the reality that there's more to most everything than that which meets the eye. (It is always the "third eye" that sees best.)

I didn't know, then, that for generations others had been similarly taken with Ojai. Artists, potters, musicians, and writers gravitated to the region. Ojai also became a leading center of theosophy when an early leader of that philosophical movement, one Albert Warrington, settled there—having noted that Ojai "was impregnated with occult and psychic influences."

So, with anticipation for revisiting Ojai *and* the possibility of scoring some lunch, we headed into town. Before we got very far, however, the latter issue was resolved. Deer Lodge, a rustic bar and restaurant that's been serving the locals since 1932, was right around a corner, and just the sort of place that jibed with my recollected visions of the territory. Without looking any further, we settled in. It was appropriately cool and dark inside, the beer was appropriately cold, and the BLT delicious, three-plus stars out of a possible four.

After that satisfying interlude we cruised into town, walked the main street, visited the tourist bureau and, finally, spent a delightful couple of hours in what has to be one of the most charming—and intelligent—bookstores in the nation. Bart's Corner, a rambling maze of indoor and outdoor shelves, has been serving Ojai readers since 1964

*I felt I must draw this sheer, plunging escarpment where purplish-gray cliffs shine in the sun along the Sespe Gorge. Herb and I are absorbed scanning the heavens for condor. We think we spot one far, far off. After all, this is the condor's realm, so I feel justified in adding one to the scene.*

and, unlike the mega-bookstores, is a haven more for lovers of books than for buyers of books. Bart's alone makes Ojai worth the trip.

We left town on Route 33. Two miles down the road, in Mira Monte, we turned right onto Route 150 and were quickly back into the country.

Route 150 meanders for sixteen miles or so to the southwest, past Lake Casitas and down to Carpinteria. As we approached the coast, the temperature eased and the scene changed—from golden hills to the lush green tropics. There were nurseries, avocados, citrus, berries, gardens, and even banana trees.

Having enjoyed the liveliness of downtown Oceanside, we chose, on approaching Carpinteria, to do the same. We turned left on Palm Avenue and finished the route on the city's bustling State Beach.

There are plenty of places to eat in Carpinteria, but when we asked after the possibility of some good Italian food we were directed a few miles up the coast to the Trattoria Palazzio, in Montecito. Back, now, in upscale territory, we celebrated a most successful day with fresh Pacific mussels, pasta, and some adequate red wine from the Old Country.

## SOME PLACES WE LIKE

✗ El Toreo restaurant. There are two El Toreos in Palmdale; this is the one on West Tenth Street. (661) 273-4050.

✗ Antelope Valley California Poppy State Reserve; (661) 724-1180.

✗ Deer Lodge; 2261 Maricopa Highway, on the outskirts of Ojai; (805) 646-4256.

✗ Bart's Corner bookstore (new and used books); 302 West Matilija, Ojai; (805) 646-3755.

✗ Trattoria Palazzio; 1151 Coast Village Road, Montecito; (805) 969-8565.

*The waves of the sea scrub the sandy shoreline of Carpinteria State Beach. Pelicans and gulls glide overhead. White sand dunes topped with green iceplant and trees fringe the extensive, well-kept beach.*

*Chapter Three*

SANTA MARIA
TO SANTA BARBARA

*From agriculture
to ultra culture.*

*About 75 miles—a lazy
half day.*

# SANTA MARIA TO SANTA BARBARA

Always interested in the state's less-traveled coastal
regions, we decided to explore the environs of the beautiful
Santa Ynez Valley. To do so, we started in Santa Maria—a
town as little known as Palmdale—and set off to
the southeast, toward Santa Barbara.
Santa Maria, though only fifty miles by direct
route from Santa Barbara, is worlds apart from
that luxurious coastal paradise.

*The Chapel of San Ramon sits on a rise of ground where country roads intersect. I draw, and
the process is like familiar handwriting, placing a collection of symbols down, telling the story of where I have
been. I notice I draw the tower on the right side of the chapel a bit cockeyed. No matter. The variance simply
adds interest to the picture. Is the church tower really that way? You will have to take the route to find out.*

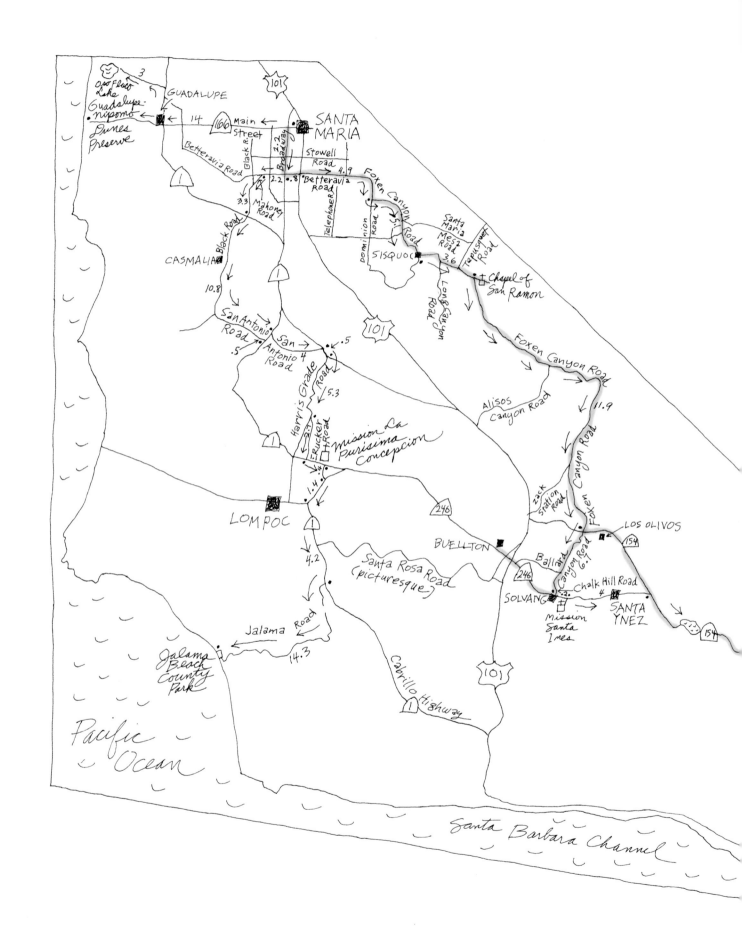

Set in the middle of thousands of acres of high-tech farms, Santa Maria is a no-nonsense city with a significant Latino population; nothing fancy, but definitely interesting—with its agriculture and proximity to some lesser-known coastal scenes. Earl and I were to spend far more time in the area than we imagined we might, and finished with a selection of three different routes out of Santa Maria.

We headed, first, for the Santa Ynez Valley's beautiful rolling ranchlands. Starting in town, we drove south on Broadway (Route 135), where there are a number of motels, turned east on Betteravia Road and then onto Foxen Canyon Road, which we followed for twenty miles or so to the southeast. There are farms along the road, growing everything from gladiolus to grapes, even some small wineries (how do they survive this far from the madding crowd?), but it's mostly horse and cattle country.

Along the way we stopped at the delightful Chapel of San Ramon. Constructed of wood and of a later era than the missions, it sits on a little knoll all by itself, looking more New England than California. While Earl sketched, I walked, and along the way encountered a young rancher who was fixing fences. We chatted, and in passing I declared that it was a mighty beautiful day.

He looked me rancher-square in the eye and declared that "*every* day's a beautiful day out here!"

Adjacent to the driveway up to the chapel is a sign to the Rancho Sisquoc Winery. There are thirty-some wineries in Santa Barbara County, quite a few along the Foxen Canyon corridor. Many are pleasant venues for picnicking. We had heard of many of the wineries in the region, the likes of Byron, Zaca Mesa, Cambria, and Foxen, but never this one—and decided to take a look. It's located, along with the fine old rancho's homes and barns, on the only intact Spanish land grant in California. The two miles of driveway (rather more than the wines) are worth the detour. There are hundreds of new olive trees, magnificent old oaks (topped by common ravens and red-tailed hawks), and some huge bulls in the fenced pastures. It is a very impressive, very California, scene.

The road dead-ends at the rancho, so you have to backtrack to Foxen Canyon Road, which then bends to the south and intersects with Route 154. Here there are a couple of options, depending on the state of your hunger or thirst or interest in the bizarre. If hungry *and* interested, proceed straight ahead onto Ballard Canyon Road and down to Solvang.

Solvang, a rather extraordinary assembly of pseudo-Scandinavian cottages and curlicues purveying all manner of sweets and curios, was created out of nothing by the Danish-American Corporation in 1911. It has out-Denmarked Denmark. Indeed, since my first visit it has out-Solvanged Solvang. It's difficult to describe, and if you've never seen it, it is definitely a must. You will certainly be able to satisfy your hunger and thirst and most particularly your sweet tooth. We managed to restrain ourselves in that department, but did walk for a while, watching the considerable throng of multinational tourists enjoying themselves.

*I have come to realize that drawing can make a location unforgettable. The bells, crosses, archways, tile roofs, and cacti here at Mission Santa Inés become real to an extent not realized if you were to simply walk by or hesitate briefly to photograph.*

Earl then moved on to work in a more austere setting, the nearby Mission Santa Inés. Earl loves to do fine detail work in his drawings—shingles, outdoor markets, leaves, and such—but the fulmination of frills in Solvang was too much, even for him. I set off to gas up the car, which took a while. I couldn't find a plain old filling station midst the cottages, so I drove a few miles west to Buellton, where normalcy resumed.

If you decide to forgo Solvang, don't go straight onto Ballard Canyon Road at the Route 154 intersection. Instead, turn left, heading southeast on 154 toward Santa Barbara. In less than a mile you're in Los Olivos. Could there be a prettier name for a town than Los Olivos, "the olive trees"?

I remember the Los Olivos of 1970 as being little more than a dirt road intersection. It isn't anymore. Around that time, the Santa Ynez Valley, not surprisingly, considering its compelling landscape, became a

hot ticket. The well-heeled of Santa Barbara and elsewhere—musicians, actors, and future presidents (i.e., Ronald Reagan)—started purchasing hideaway ranches in the valley. As is always the case, however, the word spread and more newcomers arrived. Some, the likes of actor Fess Parker and the Firestones (the tire family), planted vineyards and started producing some pretty good wines, to be followed by many more folks with that in mind.

Los Olivos, though still lovely, has passed the point of no return and is now a "destination." And that's OK, for it retains much of the charm of its setting. And whereas there was hardly anything here for anybody in the old days (unless, maybe, you were a horse), there's now something for everyone.

There are a number of attractive old buildings scattered about the town, one of which—currently housing Massimi's Ristorante—has been a local gathering place for generations. And then there's Mattei's Tavern, on the north edge of town, perhaps the most impressive structure in the territory. Built in 1886, Mattei's was a stage stop from 1861 to 1901, and even kept a few stages running until 1914 when, alas, the world changed, and the stages were retired—in favor of Model Ts. The tavern has a dark interior that appears to have changed hardly at all since the stagecoach era, and a lovely, airy, glassed-in dining porch. The pre–Model T era also gets its

due at an interesting museum in the nearby town of Santa Ynez—the Parks–Janeway Carriage House.

After taking a look around the Los Olivos–Santa Ynez neighborhood, we continued on Route 154 through attractive hilly country, toward Santa Barbara, passing along the way the scenic and substantial Lake Cachuma. There are picnic tables at Lake Cachuma, and the pull-outs here and there by the lake might be good venues for scanning the sky for condors. One of the release points for the birds raised in captivity was in Cuyama, some thirty miles (as the condor flies) to the north.

*All but obscured by vines and trees,*
*as if in voluntary hiding from our newly*
*computer-paced world, is Mattei's Tavern,*
*historic reminder of where the world has been.*

From Lake Cuchama, the hills evolve into the Santa Ynez Mountains and require a climb and then a steep descent from San Marcos Pass to Santa Barbara and the sea. Entering from this—most dramatic—direction, one appreciates the unusual, almost tropical microclimate of this stretch of the coast.

Earl and I tend to avoid large cities but, as Santa Barbara is interesting and beautiful, we decided it deserved a visit. (There was also the pressing matter of Earl's ink supply running on empty.)

So, after our formal arrival on Santa Barbara's impressive shores, we found an art shop, scored some ink, walked a while, spent some time at the Santa Barbara Mission, and eventually departed by way of the signed route through the upscale Hope Ranch neighborhood. *That* is an experience. There are so many spectacular sparkling-white homes and green lawns and palms and gardens that it must take armies of painters and arborists and gardeners (and more than a few dollars) to keep it so pristine. It is indeed somewhat overwhelming for us common people, but what the hell, it's worth a look. Imagine, for a moment, being on the Côte d'Azur, surrounded by the homes of kings in exile, princesses and stars, shipping barons and masters of the universe—and then move along, back to the real world.

## SOME PLACES WE LIKE

✘ Foxen Canyon Wine Trail; (800) 331-3779.

✘ Massimi's Ristorante; 2375 Alamo Pintado Avenue, Los Olivos; (805) 688-1941.

✘ Mattei's Tavern; Highway 154, Los Olivos; (805) 688-4820.

✘ Parks–Janeway Carriage House; 3596 Sagunto, Santa Ynez; (805) 688-7889.

*The expanse of green in front of the Santa Barbara Mission becomes ideal kiting ground. It takes a while to draw all the details in front of me. Time seems to stand still until body parts begin to ache, reminding me I have been too long in the sketching position.*

*Chapter Four*

## SANTA MARIA TO THE DUNES AND OSO FLACO LAKE

*A number of surprises
along some unknown coast.*

*A round trip of 45 miles—
only a few hours.*

With sand blowing about in the chilling wind, I prefer to draw from inside the car. Here at Nipomo is an oddly compelling landscape of sandy hillocks topped by the brave plants that volunteer to grow in such circumstances. It is an other-worldly place.

# SANTA MARIA TO THE DUNES
## AND OSO FLACO LAKE

Our next excursion out of Santa Maria was a short one. Earl and I knew nothing about the Guadalupe-Nipomo Dunes Preserve, but as it sounded intriguing, off we went, west on Main Street (Route 166). En route, into a stiff onshore breeze and the setting sun, we drove through Guadalupe, a good-sized town with a mostly Latino core and high-tech agricultural environs. It's worth looking around—it takes only minutes—for Guadalupe is evocative of the Latino experience in California. While less than picturesque,

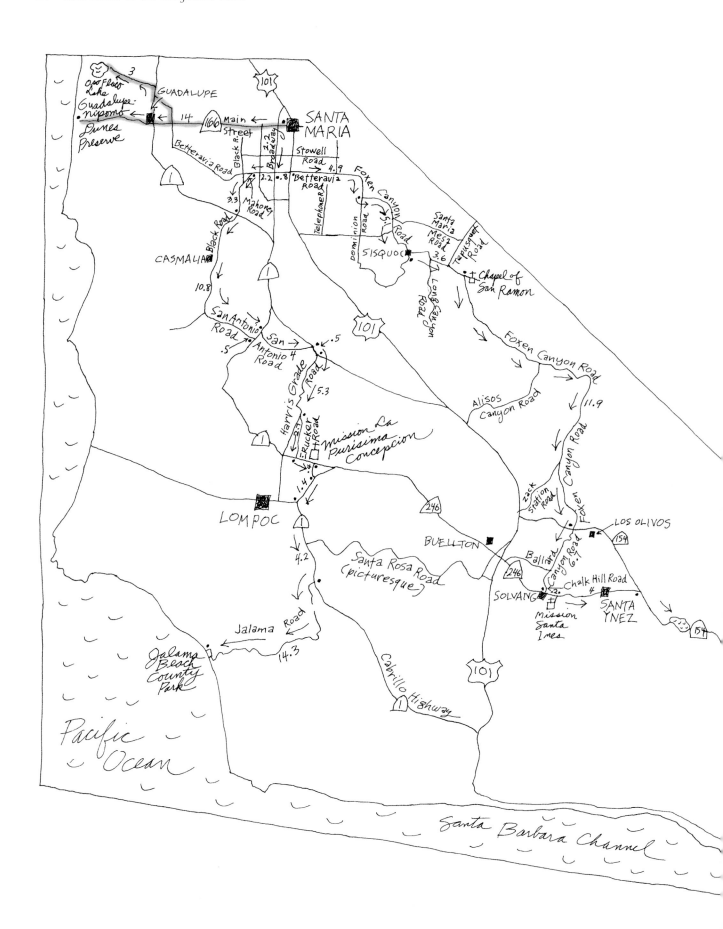

Oso Flaco Lake

3

GUADALUPE

Guadalupe-nipomo
Dunes Preserve

101

14

166 Main Street

Betteravia Road

Black R.

2.2 Broadway

SANTA MARIA

Stowell Road 4.9

2.2 .8 Betteravia Road

Foxen Canyon Road

Telephone Rd

Dominion Road

3.3 Mahoney Road

.5

Santa Maria Mesa Road

Tepusquet Road

SISQUOC

Black Road

3.6

Long Canyon Road

† Chapel of San Ramon

CASMALIA

1

10.8

Foxen Canyon Road

San Antonio Road

101

San Antonio Road

.5 .5

Alisos Canyon Road

11.9

Harris Grade

.5

5.3

Foxen Canyon Road

2.7 Jrucker Road

† Mission La Purisima Concepcion

1

zack Station Road

.4

1.4

246

LOMPOC

BUELLTON

Ballard

Los Olivos

154

4.2

246

6.7 Canyon Road

Chalk Hill Road

Santa Rosa Road (picturesque)

SOLVANG .2 †

.4

SANTA YNEZ

Jalama Road

Mission Santa Ines

154

14.3

Jalama Beach County Park

Cabrillo Highway

101

*Pacific Ocean*

*Santa Barbara Channel*

it's lively, and seems, with its new, affordable housing, to be a confident and comfortable town.

Continuing on to the west, it's a only few miles to Rancho-Guadalupe County Park, which manages the southern part of the preserve. You check in at an unpretentious little gatehouse by a long row of trees. We introduced ourselves to gatekeeper Tina (whom we came to know and appreciate over the next few days) and moved on. Very quickly the greenery gives way to sand, a great deal of sand. It's impressive, quite beautiful, and of another world. There are fields of sand, sand dunes, sand ridges, and sweeping sandy vistas down to the Santa Maria River, which meanders through a corridor of green to the sea.

Very soon, however, there was too much sand. We were driving through sand. And then more sand. And more. With our car rather low-slung and humbly two-wheel driven, I began to wonder if we could make it. It wasn't so much the sand already there as that continuing to swoop across, and settle onto, the road. I parked, and while I walked a ways to consider the risks and benefits of continuing, Earl hid in a lee and sketched this fascinating scene.

It seemed to my active imagination that the road was disappearing before my eyes, but a pickup zoomed through from the other direction, showing the sand to be only a

few inches deep. So we got back into the car and continued. However, the next pickup was slithering about in deeper sand—and that was it for us (or at least for this designated driver).

Still, we had already seen enough of the place to want to return. And return we did, a few days later, to see if we could make it through to the sea. Alas, the gate was closed, and Tina informed us that the parking lot at the end of the road had been wiped out by a rogue wave the night before. Hence the park was shut down. Maybe tomorrow?

We returned to Santa Maria and for the first time, really, had a good look around this obviously growing and successful city. After driving about in some of its newer neighborhoods, we decided to look for a place to dine in *old* Santa Maria, and near the center of town came across the original Santa Maria Inn ("The Inn That's Always Been In")—well hidden behind its new multistoried and hard-to-miss addition. It's a place of considerable charm. Stained glass, paneled walls, subdued lighting, ceiling fans, mirrored pillars, and gentle background music contribute to an increasingly rare commodity in restaurants these days: peace and quiet. The dinner wasn't quite up to the ambience, but it suited the place and was pleasantly served.

On the morrow we returned yet again to the dunes. No change, but Tina told us we were welcome to walk on in if we were so inclined. We did so and retraced the route of our windblown day. We didn't have time to go all the way to the sea, but did see plenty of deer and birds, a single coyote, and another source of the preserve's charms, Ten Commandments Hill.

For reasons known only to him, Cecil B. DeMille chose the Nipomo Dunes as the setting for his 1923 epic, *The Ten Commandments*. A giant set and huge statues of sphinxes and of Ramses the Magnificent were constructed and then, following completion of the film, buried beneath the sands—where they remain. The park doesn't advertise the presence of these relics, and would, I'm sure, prefer that C.B. had chosen some other venue, but it's all still there, with just enough bits and pieces showing atop a hill to offer a clue as to its location. (There have been plans by some archeocinematologists to excavate the ruins, but nothing yet has come of that.)

As we made our way back to the car, Tina appeared in her pickup, told us to hop in, and took us to the sea. From the looks of the ex–parking lot, it was clear she had been wise to close the gate. Along the beach and by the nearby mouth of the Santa Maria River were birds by the hundreds, and folks at the beach told us we had missed whales, close in, by only a few minutes.

After Tina returned us to our car, we drove back to Highway 1 (which also serves as the main street of Guadalupe) and turned to the north. Four miles up the road, a left turn takes you to Oso Flaco Lake. We drove in, paid our three-dollar senior fee, and discovered another coastal gem.

The lake, fringed with reedy greenery and seemingly out of place midst the sand, is a magnet for wildlife.

On the way to the lake, there's a lane through a strip of marshy woods that was, at least the day we were there, teeming with land birds. At the edge of the lake we were met by a couple of friendly raccoons—and by signs warning us that we might also meet up with a mountain lion or two. We thought that extremely unlikely, in such sandy coastal surroundings. Even in prime mountain lion country, seeing one is a rarity.

A wonderful new wheelchair-accessible walkway leads across the lake, which was loaded with waterfowl. A trail out to the beach provides another great route to the sea.

Be watchful—and careful—when exploring the coast in this region. Two of California's most endangered birds, least terns and snowy plovers, breed on beaches and dunes and are in danger of being overwhelmed by the increasing number of people, vehicles, and predators who visit the area.

Following our first trip to the area, we mentioned to friends that we'd been through Guadalupe a number of times, and they said that surely, then, we must have eaten at the Far Western Tavern. We had not. We *had* seen a number of places featuring, logically enough, Mexican food, and others pushing "Genuine Spanish food," pizza, espresso, and—less logically—"Chicago Chop Suey," but we'd missed the marquee of the tavern.

We didn't make that mistake again. As it was Saturday, we called ahead and booked for dinner. It was lucky we did. The place was booming: a full-house wedding party upstairs and a full-house restaurant and bar downstairs. It was chaotic, but it was organized chaos, and we were soon seated in the last two empty chairs in the dining room.

The Far Western shouldn't be missed: flocked wallpaper, cowhide drapes held back by horseshoes, lariats, stained glass, stuffed heads, grapevine wreaths (something, obviously, for everyone), longhorns, etchings of cattle and other creatures, and a multiethnic crowd to match. There were geezers and babies, cowboy hats, caps frontward and back, bald heads and dreadlocks.

It came as no surprise that the place is a feeder ("The Home Of The Famous Bull's Eye Steak"). It was also no surprise that the prices were right. That the food was so good *was* a bit of a surprise: this establishment is clearly more serious about the food and, for that matter, the whole show, than first impressions might suggest. A very good time was had by all.

## SOME PLACES WE LIKE

✗ Rancho-Guadalupe County Park, (805) 343-2052.

✗ Santa Maria Inn; 801 South Broadway, Santa Maria; (805) 928-7777.

✗ Far Western Tavern; Guadalupe and Ninth Street, Guadalupe; (805) 343-2211.

✗ The Santa Maria Valley Visitor and Convention Bureau offers a Central Coast Birding Trail map and general information on the wildlife of the area; (800) 331-3779.

*Chapter Five*

~

# SANTA MARIA TO JALAMA BEACH COUNTY PARK

*An easy run past farms, fields, and flowers to an out-of-the-way park.*

*About 55 miles—a half day or less.*

We left Santa Maria by heading south on Broadway, then turned right (west) on Betteravia Road. Shortly thereafter we followed a series of roads that took us first past the local farms and then into the hills.

Our first diversion was a quick look at the one-lane village of Casmalia, just off Black Road, where there were many exuberantly friendly dogs but no people. Farther along, on the Harris Grade Road in the Purisima Hills,

*I sit in shade allowing the action of drawing to free my mind and invite meditation.*
*My thoughts transport me to the time when Mission La Purisima Concepción*
*was a functioning entity. There probably were sheep and crops and*
*Indians and church bells and the creaking of horse-drawn*
*carts. Drawing excites the imagination and seems to be a*
*necessary part of my life.*
*Wherever I go, I draw.*
*We are happy travelers,*
*my pen and I.*

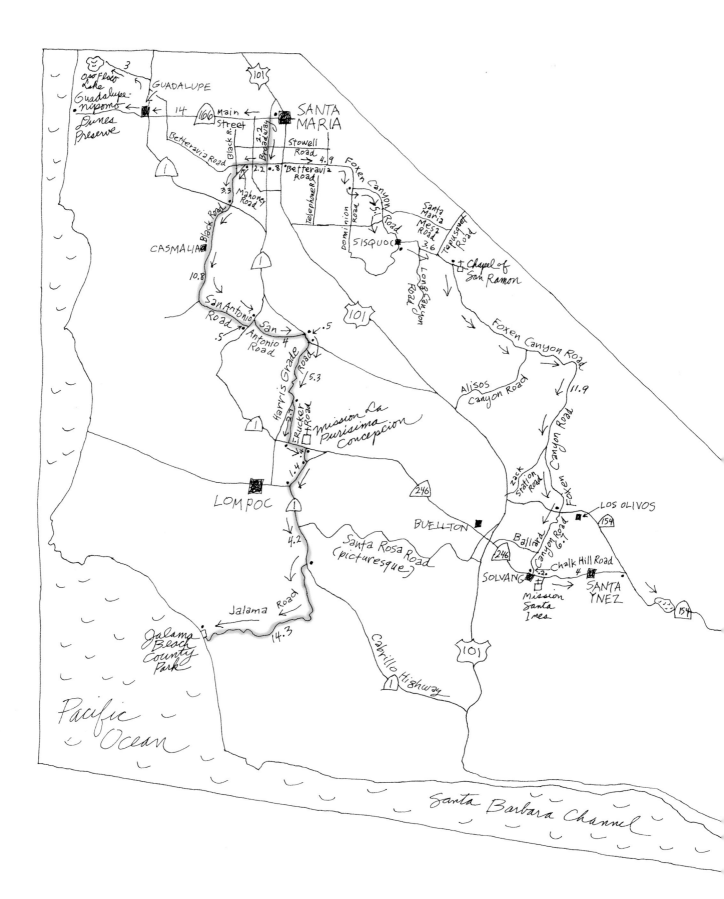

we passed through the old Lompoc Oil Field—which seemed in an odd place for an oil field. (Petroleum geology is, however, not one of my strong points.) On our travels we've often been surprised, on rounding a corner or dropping into a valley, to see clusters of oil wells. Most are inactive, but there's an occasional lonely pump jack rocking along. Sometimes these are an insult to the landscape, but at other times they can elicit from a boring vista an evocation of history and American know-how—or a visual exclamation point that seems just right.

Rucker Road cuts off to the left from the Harris Grade and runs down to Purisima Road. There's a sign at the corner to Mission La Purisima Concepción, which is about a mile to the east on Purisima Road.

La Purisima is the only one of California's twenty-one missions to have been completely restored, in the sense that the main and ancillary buildings, gardens, farms, and grounds are, as best can be determined, much as they were nearly two hundred years ago. The restoration, principally by the federal government, was a massive project, as the mission compound is vast and time had taken its toll. Originally encompassing 350,000 acres (over 500 square miles!), the compound is now restricted to the area surrounding the mission buildings—but still measures nearly 2,000 acres.

There are flower and vegetable gardens, goats, turkeys, horses, cows, pigs, and donkeys—everything

a proper farm should include. And for the active crowd, there are miles of trails in the wilds behind the mission. While we were wandering about we encountered groups of adults and youngsters running and jogging, bicyclists, walkers, and even a couple of birders. What with the variety of trees, flowers, and fountains, the birding was excellent. In the time it took for Earl to sketch the mission, I ticked off twenty species, including a mystery hummingbird.

The environs of the mission are, in a very different sort of way, just as interesting. In Lompoc, the U.S. government runs Club Fed, the prison for distinguished felons, and over at Vandenberg Air Force Base they shoot rockets up into the beyond.

Farmers in the region are involved in their own spectrum of pursuits. Particularly pleasing were the fields of incredibly brilliant flowers—acres of yellow here, blue and crimson there. Just one of these plots could change a vast and arid scene into something extraordinary. We soon learned that these fields are the most visible manifestation of this region's status as one of the world's leading producers of flower seeds.

We left Lompoc to the south on Highway 1, which behaves rather oddly hereabouts. Indeed, the roads in and around Lompoc are confusing, but you can't get *really* lost. It's one of those situations where there are a number of ways to get where you're going. Just have your map(s) handy.

After a few miles on Highway 1, we turned west onto Jalama Road. It's fourteen miles from here to the sea, a beautiful drive through rolling hills, gulches, and wonderful groves of live oaks. The drive itself is worth the drive, but so is Jalama Beach County Park.

Earl and I were just sort of drifting along, admiring the countryside, when, so to speak, we hit the beach. We immediately had the impression that we were invading a private enclave whose inhabitants would be just as happy if we didn't publicize the place. The twenty-three-acre park and beach are situated on an otherwise cliffy and deserted stretch of the coast, with no indication of civilization anywhere that we could see. The impression is that of being at the end of the world, West Coast style.

Though the population of the park changes from day to day—stays are limited and vacationers do have to return to work, and kids to school—you get the impression that, given their druthers, they'd never leave. That impression was fostered by the apparent permanence of some of the campsites and RV setups. All of the 110 spaces were taken and the place hummed with activity: ballgames on the TVs, kids on scooters, kites,

surfers, and six-packs. There's a little store and a grill—nothing special, but enough to fulfill one's basic needs until it's absolutely necessary to return to civilization.

All of that activity was too frenetic for Earl, so he climbed a distant dune and sketched from afar. I meandered about the park, trying to share in the vacation spirit of the place, but we were working people, not beach potatoes. We headed back to Santa Maria, and then toward home.

This was the last of our three excursion routes out of Santa Maria. We left with fond memories. What started out as a cursory

*There are a number of coast live oaks along the road to Jalama Beach County Park. They are decorative with thick foliage and soft gray and silvery-colored trunks.*

*Coast wind is buffeting me here at Jalama Beach, lifting my drawing paper. I can hear children yelling and dogs barking from the beach. Even though sketching is a sedentary activity, fingertips, forearm, shoulder, neck, eyes, brain, and heart are all involved. I see life. I hear life and I am a part of it.*

look at the region had evolved into quite an experience, the result of our being so impressed with Santa Barbara, the Nipomo Dunes, Oso Flaco Lake, and Jalama Beach—a good example of serendipity and traveling without a plan.

On looking at the map, it's obvious that these three routes out of Santa Maria are perfect for mixing and matching. There are many opportunities for circular trips and alternate routes throughout the region. It just depends on how much time is available and your preferences in accommodations and food.

Something that rendered all these adventures particularly enjoyable was their understated and spontaneous nature. When you go to Yosemite or Big Sur or Disneyland, you know exactly what to expect: rogue waves and sandstorms and confusing roads aren't going to alter your daily schedule.

## A PLACE WE LIKE

✘ Jalama Beach County Park; (805) 736-6316; www.sbparks.com.

*Chapter Six*

## BAKERSFIELD TO
### MORRO BAY

*A little bit of
everything on a fine
and peaceful road.*

*About 150 miles—most
of a day.*

*From the elevated viewpoint, to the accompaniment*
*of busily engaged, buzzing flies, I sketch the silent, glistening-white Soda Lake*
*in all its vast, horizontal splendor. Then Herb shows me a wanted sign posted*
*nearby. He knows of my approval. It states that "Star Thistle" is "Wanted +*
*Wanted Dead." Here are the crimes it has committed: "Choking etc."*

# BAKERSFIELD TO MORRO BAY

When you think about it, almost any road in California must connect
with a road that connects with a road that connects with a road that leads to
the sea, so we started this route in a somewhat unlikely place.
One does not think much about soaring gulls and crashing surf in Bakersfield
and, admittedly, Route 58 just west of the city is not evocative of same.
It does take a while, but after it gets going, 58 is a jewel.

In truth, you *could* start west of Bakersfield in Buttonwillow—perhaps for no other reason than its name. Or in the oil town of McKittrick. You should certainly take a look at McKittrick, not for its charm, but for its drilling rigs, pump jacks, pipes, tanks, and all its other arcane industrial paraphernalia. (This is probably a guy thing.)

Just beyond McKittrick the road climbs into the Temblor Range of hills, so named because they were created by the San Andreas Fault, which still rumbles along on the other side of the hills—aimed like an arrow at San Francisco.

After you cross the fault you're looking out over one of California's true treasures, the Carrizo Plain. The plain is, figuratively and literally, a breath of fresh air compared to what most of bigger-than-life California has to offer. In the first place, not many Californians know about it. Anyone not paying attention could drive through and hardly notice it. As a dry, high-country plateau it is as subtle as a desert.

Always interesting, the plain teems with life in the winter and spring. In the early spring a few years back I was there when it was at its best, with wildflowers and sandhill cranes on the flats and raptors patrolling overhead.

However, to test its, and our, mettle, Earl and I arrived on a 100-degree midsummer day. Immediately, a good omen: perched on a pole, checking us out, a handsome prairie falcon. There weren't many other birds and only a few flowers. But what was lost in action was gained in the sort of solitude that Earl and I appreciate.

Unless time is a factor, spend a few hours exploring the plain. As you come down from the hills, go straight ahead onto Seven Mile Road rather than northwest on Route 58. This is one of just a few dirt roads we recommend, but it's broad and flat and not a problem—except for the seasonal dust. It cuts across to Soda Lake Road, which runs along the west edge of the plain. The whole area to the southeast, which includes Soda Lake

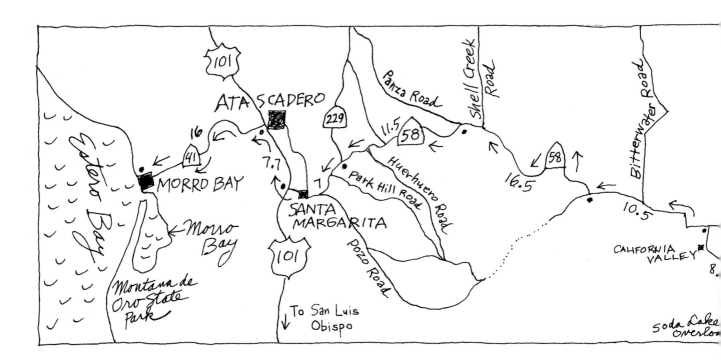

and the most interesting aspects of the plain, has been protected from development, largely through the efforts of the Nature Conservancy.

We turned left (southeast) at the Soda Lake Road intersection and drove a couple of miles to a Soda Lake overlook on the right. We saw only a bone-dry, eye-scorching, mineral-white expanse. There being no outlet for the skimpy rains of winter, what water falls on the plain collects in the lake and then evaporates, leaving the brilliant white residue. It's a unique environment, the largest remaining natural alkali wetland in California.

Earl braved this fierce and shadeless scene to sketch the dry lake from atop a knoll while I beat the bushes (so to speak, there being very few bushes, and not a tree to be seen) for the tough summer residents of the plain: a few bugs and lizards, common ravens overhead, and some panting Western meadowlarks (their wings open to the barely perceptible breeze) on a nearby bulletin board.

The board supplied considerable off-season information, most predominantly a "Wanted" poster for an unwanted encroaching resident of the plain, the nefarious yellow star thistle. This sharp-spined nonnative weed (originally from southern Europe) has invaded California and is driving ranchers, farmers, and open-space folks to distraction. To date there's not much of it on the plain, so the word is out to attack it sooner rather than later, before it overwhelms the native grasslands and wildflowers. Getting rid of it "later" is almost impossible. Earl was particularly understanding of this, for his back aches every spring from pulling up the star thistle that attempts to invade *his* property.

Farther down Soda Lake Road, again on the right, is the Guy L. Goodwin Education Center, generally open only from December 1 to June 1. The staff there will let you know what, and where, the outdoors action is. Over the course of the next few years it is hoped that the educational programs on the plain will be expanded—a result of the welcome news that

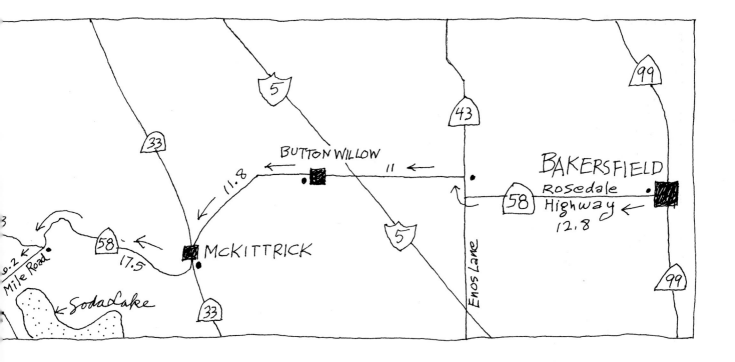

President Clinton, at the end of his term, designated the Carrizo Plain a national monument.

Drive south for a few miles and then turn around and head back up Soda Lake Road to Route 58, where you can continue to the west. For the next forty miles or so the road meanders through beautiful hill country and is just what a road should be: gently curving, following the contours of the rolling hills, and somehow never intruding into the landscape. There should be medals struck honoring those responsible for the construction of roads such as these.

Just to the west of the plain it's extremely dry—mostly grassland and junipers. However, with each mile or so, as the annual rainfall increases by a few millimeters, the junipers gradually lose out to the oaks, and the ravens to the magpies. And finally, on approaching Santa Margarita, the landscape becomes less austere.

A mile past Santa Margarita, Route 58 terminates at Highway 101. Here, there are two options, neither of the back-road variety but both worthwhile. You can go north about eight miles and head for the sea on Route 41, the busy but reasonably attractive highway between Atascadero and Morro Bay. Or you can go south through San Luis Obispo on Highway 101 and on to Avila Beach and Port San Luis. Earl and I chose to finish in Morro Bay, which overlooks Morro Rock, certainly one of the most distinctive sights on the Pacific coast.

In 1972, when I first spent some time in Morro Bay, I was so taken with it that I began to think about the Central Coast as a permanent place to settle down. There were fish houses down at the harbor and birds flying, diving, and swimming everywhere. And the huge rock itself held a hallowed place in the heart of every California birder as home to one of the few breeding pairs of the state's peregrine falcons.

The bay still teems with life. A couple of years ago I sat and watched three or four California sea lions consume a prodigious number of very large octopi in the space of fifteen minutes, while huge flocks of local birds competed for the leavings.

The whole area in and around Morro Bay is a nature preserve—almost a seaside zoo. There are inland parks and, along the coast, Morro Strand State Beach to the

*I'm on a cliff overlooking Morro Rock, next to an ancient cypress that must have been here when only Indians lived along the misty coast. Morro Rock is off in the distance, shrouded in banks of snowy-colored fog.*

north and the very considerable Montana de Oro State Park to the south.

But you also can't go wrong if you choose to turn south from Route 58 and take the San Luis Obispo route to the sea. San Luis is one of California's most perfect cities: beautifully situated, with a great climate, a mission, a college, some excellent restaurants, and the world's weirdest motel, the multithemed and altogether over-the-top Madonna Inn.

About eight miles south of San Luis on Highway 101—just before you get to the overdeveloped series of towns running from Shell Beach down to Oceano State Beach—you can turn off to the west and head through some beautiful, though rapidly developing, countryside into Avila Beach and Port San Luis. These two bayside settlements are quite

unlike any others in our collection. To me, Port San Luis looks more Alaska than California. It is, for the most part, a huge long pier sticking out into San Luis Obispo Bay, surrounded ashore by the typical trappings of the boating and fishing industry—including flocks of gulls and fleets of noisy California sea lions.

On the other hand, Avila Beach is heading upscale. There's a large new resort nearby and considerable development action downtown. The transition from funky to fashionable was, for Avila Beach, not exactly of its own doing. In a dramatic 1999 response to the revelation that Union Oil Company of California had leaked some 400,000 gallons of toxics into the soil beneath the town, downtown Avila Beach was leveled and cleaned up. The recent infusion of funds by Union Oil and the state has resulted in the town's new and handsome look. Sometimes, miracles *do* happen!

## A PLACE WE LIKE

 Guy L. Goodwin Education Center; on the Carrizo Plain near Soda Lake; (805) 475-2717.

*Chapter Seven*

## TULARE TO CAMBRIA

*135 direct,
or 165 meandering,
miles, from the
Central Valley to
the Central Coast.*

*A short day (direct) or a
long day (meandering).*

In the tiny San Joaquin Valley village of Stratford, I draw the curious park that is on the east end of town in the middle of the main street. There is a similar park and sign also on the west end of town. Roosters are crowing, a loudspeaker blaring, early morning sunshine on my back—small farm barn, big farm buildings, and right in the middle of the place, quaint Mexican-American homes.

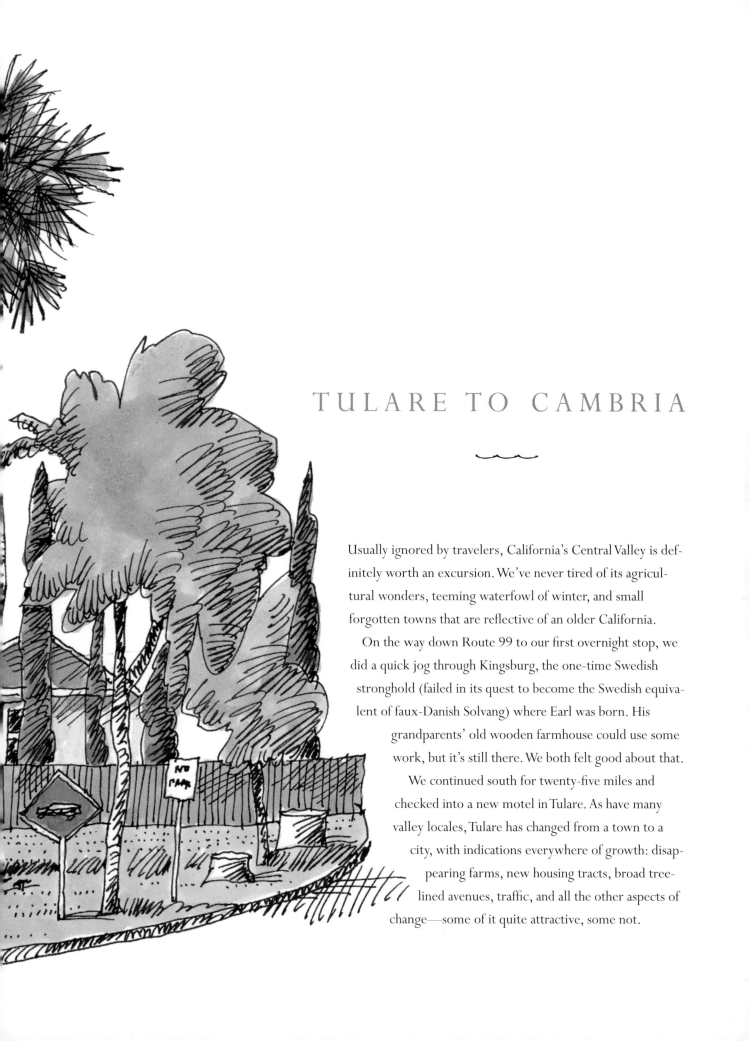

# TULARE TO CAMBRIA

Usually ignored by travelers, California's Central Valley is definitely worth an excursion. We've never tired of its agricultural wonders, teeming waterfowl of winter, and small forgotten towns that are reflective of an older California.

On the way down Route 99 to our first overnight stop, we did a quick jog through Kingsburg, the one-time Swedish stronghold (failed in its quest to become the Swedish equivalent of faux-Danish Solvang) where Earl was born. His grandparents' old wooden farmhouse could use some work, but it's still there. We both felt good about that.

We continued south for twenty-five miles and checked into a new motel in Tulare. As have many valley locales, Tulare has changed from a town to a city, with indications everywhere of growth: disappearing farms, new housing tracts, broad tree-lined avenues, traffic, and all the other aspects of change—some of it quite attractive, some not.

But we were less concerned with aesthetics than with other matters. It had been a long drive, so we were, of course, hungry—but on the basis of past experience in the valley, not hopeful. As is the case, however, for the upside of growth and development, there now *is* hope. At the motel, some folks who clearly knew their way around Tulare were able to tell us about a number of places where we might eat reasonably well.

So we headed downtown and dined at V's, an establishment that would have been beyond the wildest, most grandiose fantasies of the dust-bowlers who settled in Tulare. The closest thing to it would be the poolroom at the Big Apple's Four Seasons done up in dark velvet with bordello overtones. For an hour, Earl and I were the only customers, enthroned in a huge banquette and surrounded by a near-bevy of delightful young Tularian servers. We weren't encouraged by the surroundings and the menu—but the meal was absolutely delicious! Amazing. Good salads to start, Earl's steak was the best California beef I'd ever tasted, and my spaghetti puttanesca would've held its own with The Four Seasons'.

Only on the rarest occasions have we insisted upon meeting a chef in order to convey praise. This was one of them. And it was the first time the chef was a she. Not only a she, but young,

bright, articulate, well-trained (at the Napa Valley Cooking School) and, as best we could tell, eminently sane. How times have changed in the country's kitchens!

The next morning, feeling enthused about the Central Valley, we set off, dead straight west on Route 137, and then Kansas Avenue, to Route 41. Again, agribusiness on a grand scale, with huge dairy barns and the almost-mansions of successful farmers. Between the dairies: orchards and vast fields of corn and cotton.

Before leaving the area, we thought we should have a look at the "other" Central Valley, so we spent some time in Stratford, just south of the Kansas Avenue/Route 41 intersection. Very much the antithesis of booming Tulare (and other cities along the Route 99 corridor), Stratford is the sort of small, quiet, mostly Latino town that supplies the troops who do the dirt work on the valley farms.

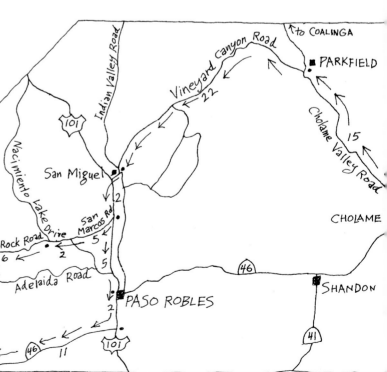

There is, at first glance, not much to see—just the usual *mercado,* auto parts store, defunct gas station, and such—but a dividend unique to such backwaters is the opportunity to see, in the rough, some of the agricultural and architectural history of California. In the Tulares of this world, with their inexorable push for the new and efficient, anything not measuring up is torn down and replaced. In the Stratfords, they're left to die of their own accord, at their own pace. Hence, around the edges of Stratford are the remains of several eras of agricultural architecture, some quite enigmatic as to their onetime function, a couple quite handsome.

If you're not interested in Tulare and the stretch of road to the west of it, you can pick up this route from Interstate 5. From the north, get on Route 41 at its intersection with I-5 near Kettleman City. From the south, you can get off I-5 near Lost Hills and take Route 46 for thirty-seven miles west to its junction with 41.

Whichever the approach, both 41 and 46 start off on the agricultural flats, move west through oil country, climb over their respective passes, descend across the San Andreas Fault, and merge just east of the tiny settlement of Cholame (pronounced SHOW-lamb). Go on into Cholame.

A half-mile from here, at 5:59 P.M., on September 30, 1955, actor James Dean, driving into the sun, was killed when he crashed his Porsche Spyder—a indelible event for many of that era. There's a monument in front of Cholame's cafe, and people still show up from time to time to recall that day. Curiously, the monument was erected by a Japanese businessman, one Seita Ohnishi, whose inscription reads, in part: "In Japan, we say his death came as suddenly as it does to cherry blossoms. The petals of early spring always fall at the height of their ephemeral brilliance. Death in youth is life that glows eternal."

At this point along the route, you have a number of options. You can continue on the merged Routes 41/46, take 41 when it splits from 46 at Shandon, and follow it down to Atascadero and Morro Bay. Or you can stay on 46, through Paso Robles and down to the sea, passing the Meridian, Eberle, and other Central Coast wineries along the way.

However, as you're already out in the outback, why not bite the bullet and continue even farther into it. (If you do, make sure you have gas for a couple of hours of driving.)

From Cholame, backtrack two-tenths of a mile and turn north onto Cholame Valley Road. For the next

Map labels: 41 · Kansas Avenue ←—17 · STRATFORD · 41 18 · 5 · KETTLEMAN CITY · 33 · 8 · 41 · 20 · 46 · 137 · 137 · TULARE · 99

*Tree of Heaven at the James Dean monument at Cholame: "His death came as suddenly as it does to cherry blossoms. The petals of early spring always fall at the height of their ephemeral brilliance."*
—Seita Ohnishi, September 30, 1977.

JAMES DEAN
1931 Feb: — 1955 Sep 30 pm 5:59 ∞

fifteen miles or so, you'll be traveling, together with the San Andreas Fault, up the beautiful Cholame Valley. It's classic Western range and ranch land, always with at least some wildflowers—and maybe a golden eagle or two. The valley runs up to "The Shakiest Town in America," Parkfield.

Though not picturesque and indeed quite funky, tiny Parkfield (population 30-odd) is worth a special journey. Sitting plunk upon the fault, with a history of multiple shakes and shocks and aftershocks, it's surrounded by scientific gadgetry and is, *with enthusiasm,* awaiting the Big One. Take a look around and you'll see signs of the stresses affecting the area. The bridge leading into town has some subtle curves that don't belong, and there's a pair of markers in the village park, separated by the distance the fault has moved since the slippage was first calculated (12.4 feet since 1931).

Curiously, the *inhabitants* of Parkfield do not appear to be the least bit stressed.

There's the rustic Parkfield Inn ("Sleep here when it happens"), the Parkfield Cafe, and a tiny gift shop—all shaded by huge valley oaks and staffed by the laid-back locals. It is, somehow, a cozy scene.

While Earl busied himself sketching the bizarre fountain in the park, I walked and birded: kestrels and red-tails everywhere, and a single sunlit prairie falcon atop the tallest oak.

Now, of course, it will appear that you have driven yourself into—or, more accurately, been directed into—a shaky corner of nowhere. There are, however, three options. You can continue north on the Parkfield-Coalinga Road and Parkfield Grade to Route 198—but this would, in a big way, violate our promise to keep you to reasonably civilized roads. (Beware of "grades," a word that can mean almost anything.) Or you can turn around and return to Route 46. Or you can cross the bridge just south of town and turn right onto Vineyard Canyon Road. This twenty-five-mile country road will then take you over to the small town of San Miguel, Mission San Miguel Arcàngel and, for those

*This ingenious fountain is in the Parkfield Park.*
*No one interrupted my drawing time on a very pleasant day here. The*
*community boasts that it is the earthquake center of the world.*

*This is one of the charmingly restored older houses in old Cambria. Now they are shops and restaurants to delight the tourist.*

interested in early California structures, the Rios-Caledonia Adobe.

The mission, with its irregular arches, wonderfully frescoed interior, and generally stark exterior, is one of those few that have genuinely retained their unspoiled aura. It merits a visit.

From San Miguel it's about seven miles down Highway 101 to Paso Robles. Paso is a town-now-city of more than passing interest. In pre–Interstate 5 days, when travelers between San Francisco and Los Angeles took 101, Paso was a convenient place to break up what was usually a two-day trip. Many of us had heard of the mission-style Paso Robles Inn before we'd heard of Paso Robles. Interstate 5 took away much of that action (and, thankfully, most of the trucks), but Paso has survived. There are plenty of places to stay, a fine large plaza, and a selection of some better-than-average restaurants.

A few miles south of town, Route 46 leaves Highway 101 to the west and continues to the sea. There are now two final options:

If time is a factor, it's a quick twenty-two miles down 46 to Highway 1 and the coast. Route 46 is a beautiful road, if busy at times, and passes through miles of attractive coastal countryside.

If time is *not* a factor, you can go west of Paso Robles on Route 46 for about a dozen miles and take a right turn onto Santa Rosa Creek Road, a horse of a different color. This is most definitely a genuine back-road route for those willing to put up with a narrow and often bumpy track. It winds along year-round Santa Rosa Creek to Cambria, a sixteen-mile trip through steep and darkly shaded forest that takes a while, but will be time well spent.

Thirty years ago, Cambria was a quaint and tweedy hideaway on an isolated stretch of coast. But for Hearst Castle, it would be still. Over the years, however, because of the ever-increasing interest in the castle and, I guess, the ever-increasing number of Californians, it has sprawled a bit. It's no longer a hideaway, but there are vestiges of its past charm. Some of the old village's nineteenth-century homes have been restored; the bizarre patchwork home constructed up on Hillcrest Drive by one Arthur Beale continues (just barely) to defy gravity; and the old-timers, dressed in proper whites, regularly turn out to lawn bowl.

From Cambria it's only about a mile to coastal Highway 1. There are a number of county and state parks along this beautiful coastline, any of which would be a proper place to conclude this route. While Earl sketched, I concluded it in the parking lot at Moonstone Beach, listening to a bronzed California surfer enthrall a group of lovely young ladies with his tales of being out there when the surf was really up. He even had *me* enthralled when he spoke of how "after you've been up there, riding ten-foot waves, food tastes better than it ever has."

Just two miles south of the Route 46/Highway 1 intersection, there's a cluster of weathered old wooden buildings, the charming hamlet of Harmony. For years Harmony was famed for being "the only town in America that's for sale." In 1997 it was finally sold, the whole show: gift shop, glass works, cafe, pottery shop, and tiny wedding chapel. Among the resident artisans, there was hope for some renovation, but there has been none to date. (We sort of like it the way it is, but then again it's not our roof that's leaking.)

The tiny coastal village of San Simeon is some eight miles north of the intersection; its neighbor, Hearst Castle, perches atop a ridge in the Santa Lucia Range. There's little to say about the castle and its magnificent setting that hasn't been said before. I'm always transfixed by its two spectacular swimming pools, Earl by the intricacies of the architecture, others by the sheer dimensions of the place. There is indeed something for *everyone.* So, no matter what opinions one holds concerning William Randolph Hearst, or the manner in which he ran his business, or his taste in architecture and art, or *Citizen Kane,* the castle's a kick, and interesting no matter how many times one visits.

*These carts are traditional at California missions. Once I illustrated an American postage stamp of an early California dwelling and used a similar cart as a motif in the design.*

## OTHER ROUTES TO TRY

✗ It's possible to work your way down to Santa Rosa Creek Road and then Cambria through the maze of roads northwest of Paso Robles: San Marcos Road to Nacimiento Lake Drive, Chimney Rock Road, Adelaida Road, and Klau Mine Road. It's attractive—and interesting—back in there, but it's also easy to get lost. Both times we tried, Cypress Mountain Drive, the extension of Klau Mine Road, was under repairs and closed. Have a very good map.

✗ As is obvious on the maps, Routes 58 (Chapter 6) and 46 can be mixed and matched. Or, if you want to do a great circle, you could finish more or less where you started. How you do it depends on your own preferences, the season, the weather, available time, etc. However you do it, you'll probably pass through Cholame, but after that: Parkfield? San Miguel? Paso Robles? Atascadero? San Simeon? Morro Bay? Or all of the above?

## SOME PLACES WE LIKE

✗ V's restaurant; 210 East Tulare Street, Tulare;
(559) 684-1264.

✗ Parkfield Inn; 70410 First Street, Parkfield;
(805) 463-2424.

✗ Hearst Castle; (800) 444-4445. Reservations for
tours essential.

*The fog allowed me a glimpse of Hearst Castle along the mountain's profile. With binoculars I could see the main towers glistening when the sun appeared for a moment.*

## Chapter Eight

## KING CITY TO LUCIA

*Mission San Antonio de Padua, the Santa Lucia Mountains, and the sea.*

*About 50 miles—a half to a whole day.*

*A broad field spreads out in front of Mission San Antonio de Padua, allowing a long view of the historic edifice. Only birdsong reaches my ears. It is so quiet and tranquil.*

# KING CITY TO LUCIA

While it was impossible to choose California's *almost-best* back road to the sea, there was never any doubt as to the *best* road. And though the route is no secret, it's like a favorite restaurant: one hesitates to blow its cover for fear of opening the floodgates.

What should such a route offer? There would have to be a mission, a stretch of almost desert, a daunting road through the mountains, sundry broad vistas, a couple of decent restaurants, some local color, a proper stretch of coast, and maybe, for a dividend, some otters or whales. And it shouldn't be in anybody's backyard, too easy of access.

Given all that, there's no choice but to drive to an isolated stretch of Highway 101—roughly halfway between Salinas and Paso Robles; indeed, halfway between Mexico and Oregon—and head for the City Cafe in King City.

As Earl and I approached King City, I recounted the trip my wife and I had made there in 1970. We had been out on the coast, on Highway 1, but it was so foggy we decided, on a whim, to turn inland onto a dirt road—the Nacimiento Grade (Nacimiento-Fergusson Road). The sun broke through the fog, the temperature rose, and the road became so steep that my old car hissed and seemed about to die. We finally did make it, and after our descent to the road across the scorching Fort Hunter Liggett Military

*The inn near Mission San Antonio de Padua dominates a rise in land from the broad valley of the wildflowers.*

Reservation, we saw signs to a mission we'd never heard of—San Antonio de Padua. We decided to have a look. We were, however, in a severe state of hunger and thirst and there was no secular sustenance to be had at the mission, its only concession to the twentieth cen- tury being an ancient fountain that dribbled water hot- ter than the weather. We checked our maps, and our best bet appeared to be King City, on Highway 101, twenty miles to the east.

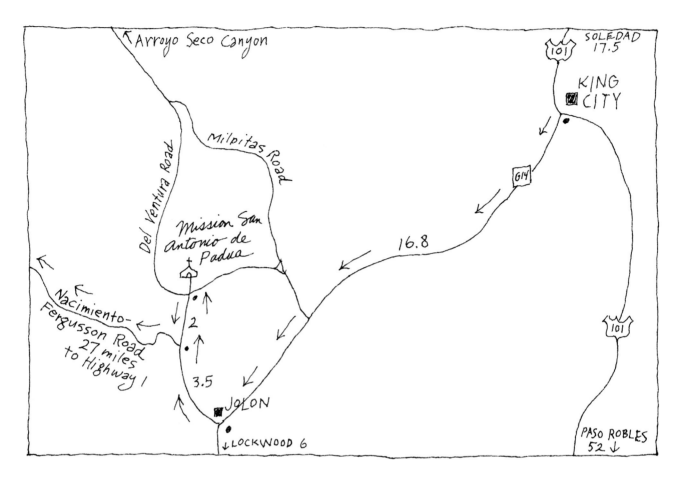

We drove over there and, for no particular reason, chose for our resuscitation the City Cafe, one of King City's numerous Mexican restaurants. It was a pleasant, cooling, healing interlude and we were soon ready to return to the mission for some spiritual resuscitation.

And now, thirty years later, I thought it appropriate, for old-times' sake, to buy Earl a meal at the City Cafe. It's difficult to define its charm, for it's *not* charming, and the food—typical Mexican American fare—though good, is hardly worth a special journey. It's neither chic nor cute, just down-home pleasant—and just right. Over the years of my occasional visits it hasn't changed: same old gumball machines, beer signs, painted velvet *Last Supper,* Aztec calendar plate, American flag, fading photo of Jack and Jackie—and same old menu. (There *has* been one addition, a sign for O'Doul's nonalcoholic beer up by the clock.)

Refreshed again, Earl and I were ready to go. First, we toured the town. Tucked out of the way, just off the Broadway exit from 101, is the San Lorenzo County Park. Running along both sides of the Salinas River, it's extensive and quite delightful, with all manner of facilities: farming museum, ball fields, picnic grounds, walking trails, and spacious lawns. There's plenty of cover and water in a region generally lacking same, so the birding can be remarkable, most any time of the year.

Along Highway 101 is the usual conglomeration of motels, fast-food establishments, and filling stations and, nearby, a new shopping center and hospital. As you move up Broadway, the scene changes, block by block. It becomes increasingly Latino, with a couple of restaurants at the far end indistinguishable from any colorful mariachi-booming cantinas south of the border.

We then left for the mission and the coast: first,

seventeen miles southwest on Route G14 to Jolon and, after a right turn onto Mission Road, about six miles to the mission.

The mission enclave is completely within Fort Hunter Liggett Military Reservation, an extraordinary place in its own right. Until the army acquired it in 1940, it was a Hearst family ranch, a quiet refuge of 165,000 acres (250-plus square miles) far from the social bustle of the castle in San Simeon. The Hacienda, its beautiful mission-style lodge designed by Julia Morgan (of Hearst Castle fame), was once the officers' club. It's still there, near the Hunter Liggett headquarters, and, wonder of wonders, is now an inn, open to the public. While not offering sophisticated fare and/or services, it's handsome, and the rooms, restaurant, and lounge are quite Hearstian in their proportions, and eminently affordable. It's best to reserve rooms months ahead if you want to visit during the spring wildflower season in March and April.

If Mission La Purisima Concepcion's grounds are the most extensive and San Antonio de Pala's sanctuary the most spiritual, de Padua has enough of these, plus its isolation, that renders it, for Earl and me anyway, the most evocative of the mission experience. The original missions were located so that each was a day's ride from the next. It was a long ride from *anywhere* to San Antonio de Padua, thirty-some miles over tough terrain from its neighbors, Missions Soledad and San Miguel. Such times, and terrain, had to have bred tough riders, and tougher horses.

Except for some thoughtful restoration, the mission had been altered little since my first visit. The problems associated with restoring California's missions are varied and complex. If restored *too* well (San Luis Obispo; Carmel; Santa Ines), they begin to look like reproductions. If you use a lighter touch, they keep

deteriorating and maintenance becomes exorbitantly expensive. Adobe, not the toughest of materials, is easily eroded by the downpours of winter. Earthquakes wreak disaster on unreinforced walls. Wooden statuary is consumed by worms. And fires.

Earl and I were at San Antonio de Padua on an early spring weekday, so we had this magical place pretty much to ourselves. After being blitzed for months by California's surfeit of faux Spanish architecture, we found it a joy to be back to the real thing. One passes through a time warp, for not much has changed in the nearly two hundred years since the mission's founding. There's nothing to detract from the reality of what the place once was, the only resting place in the middle of a vast nowhere. It was this—and the absence of the *stuff*-laden clutter of our current world—that afforded us one of those momentary perceptions of what life predominantly of the spirit once was.

After a walkabout, we settled in: Earl sketched; I wandered, checking out the scene. There were acorn woodpeckers and northern flickers in the oaks, California quail foraging in the fields, and the usual contingent of American kestrels and red-tailed hawks cruising overhead. And it was clearly going to be a banner year for lupine and poppies.

Eventually we had to move along. We hated doing so, but there were miles to go—back to the twenty-first century.

About two miles back toward Jolon, on the road we came in on, there's a right turn onto the Nacimiento-Fergusson Road. We now headed toward the coast through Hunter Liggett. (Another road south out of the mission, just to the west of the main road, also intersects with the Nacimiento-Fergusson Road. Whichever you take, make sure you cross the old bridge over the San Antonio River.)

As the Nacimiento-Fergusson Road is the only road to the coast for many miles, the military was obligated to allow traffic through the base. Hence, after absorbing the peaceful solitude of the mission, we were, within minutes, confronted by columns of thundering tanks and fearful ordnance—in their spirituality the antithesis of San Antonio de Padua. For Earl and me, who grew up during sundry American conflicts, such scenes were, despite our distaste for all things warlike, not unimpressive.

After running along the glorious oak-lined valley floor west of the mission, the road climbs three thousand feet into, up, and over the Santa Lucia Mountains and down to the sea. It's paved now and wider than it once was, but it retains its thrills.

Your reward for crossing the mountains is one of the more spectacular arrivals on any coast anywhere. And if you're lucky you can lunch in sun at the Lucia Lodge, five miles up the road, truly on the edge of the sea, in tiny Lucia.

*Oak woodlands occupy the first picturesque landscape to drive through as we move toward the California coast along the Nacimiento-Fergusson Road.*

## SOME PLACES WE LIKE

✗ City Cafe; located quite a ways up Broadway, King City's main street, just a door or two down from the now defunct Reel Joy movie house; (831) 385-9943.

✗ The Hacienda; P.O. Box 712, Jolon, CA 93928-0712; (831) 386-2900.

✗ Lucia Lodge; (831) 667-2391.

✗ The California Missions Foundation is soliciting funds to coordinate a statewide approach toward restoring and preserving the missions; 5 Third Street, San Francisco, CA 94103; (877) 632-3623; (415) 764-1616.

*Chapter Nine*

## KING CITY TO CARMEL

*A fruitful trip down the
Carmel Valley.*

*A 68-mile cruise—an easy
half day.*

# KING CITY TO CARMEL

While Earl and I were studying our maps of the King City region,
we noticed a road from nearby Greenfield that ran all the way down the Carmel
Valley. We asked about it and learned that the first twenty-five miles or so out of
Greenfield meandered through some country as wild and undeveloped as the
miles nearer the coast were not. And, as we couldn't resist a road we'd never
taken, we made a route of it.

*In bobcat (Herb spotted one) and quail country, I draw this falling-down
farm house. We are still a ways from the development creeping eastward
from Carmel Valley. I have always appreciated the fact that while
drawing I enter into the atmosphere of the location,
listening, being aware of odors, observing
and enjoying the stream of life that flows
around me, no matter how
slowly it evolves.*

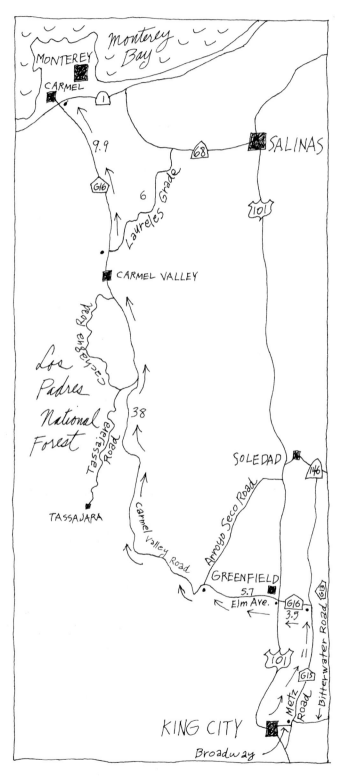

After a big breakfast at Keefer's, where they've been serving up good American food to the residents of King City for over fifty years, we drove up to Greenfield—not on Highway 101, but on Route G15, on the east side of the valley. At the G15 intersection with G16 we turned to the west.

The territory around Greenfield is completely involved in high-tech agribusiness. I know they have laser levelers and tractors with sophisticated steering mechanisms and all that, but I still don't see how they get those fields *so* flat and rows *so* straight. And I know—but don't want to know any more than I do now—about super-seeds and hybrids and insecticides and herbicides (and other-cides, no doubt), but I still cannot figure out how *every* stalk of corn is exactly the height of its siblings.

When one realizes the investment of knowledge, equipment, labor, and financial risk involved in producing a Salinas Valley head of lettuce, whatever its price in a corner grocery in, say, midwinter Utica, New York, it's got to be a bargain. (Note: Earl and I are *not* lobbyists for the American farm industry.)

We cruised through the farms and into the substantial hills of the Sierra de Salinas. Beautiful country, with oak woodlands running up the slopes and an undergrowth of native grasses and sundry wildflowers. One can travel for many curved and hilly miles before encountering the BMWs, Benzes, and ever-escalating whirl of the Monterey Peninsula scene.

Near one of the road's higher points, with views in every direction, we stopped to admire the morning and the mountains. Even though the day was already warming up, there were birds everywhere, working the edge of the road, the live oaks, and the morning thermals rising above us. (In only a few minutes, I found eighteen species, mostly of the oak tree sort—chestnut-backed chickadees, white-breasted nuthatches, oak tit-mice, Nuttall's woodpeckers, and though not particularly common in this habitat, an extraordinary number of always delightful California towhees.)

While Earl sketched a ramshackle old farmhouse, I set off along the road. After only a few minutes I heard shuffling in a nearby field, and some game birds flushed and flew. They were quail, but not the regular California quail. These were mountain quail, an often heard but rarely seen California specialty. While appreciating the moment—only my second sure sighting ever of these infernally elusive birds—I heard some "cluck-cluck-clucking" in the grass, clearly more quail. So I stopped, listened, watched, and waited.

After a while another listener and watcher appeared. The big bobcat was so preoccupied with the birds that, for five minutes or so, he failed to see me. Eventually he did, but what to do next? He chose to ignore the birds for the moment and walked toward me for a closer look. Still unsure of what to do, and obviously reluctant to give up the possibility of some nice mountain quail tartare for breakfast, he just stood there. Finally he, or she, decided to leave, but not without stopping and directing a few more perplexed glances in my direction.

Earl and I also left, but were hardly up to speed before we had to slow for a large flock of turkeys and soon thereafter a family of deer. Indeed, for our first hour we encountered more wildlife than traffic. That didn't last too much longer, for the traffic gradually increased as we approached the village of Carmel Valley.

Once a genuine village, populated by old-timers and a few others who preferred the hot valley sun over the oft-foggy coast, Carmel Valley has gone upscale. However, it's still an attractive place, with an increasing number of interesting places to eat and to stay.

As you continue down the road, you begin to notice some of the establishments for which the valley is famous, the likes of Quail Lodge, the fine Marinus Restaurant at Bernardus Lodge, the Chateau Julien Winery, and Los Laureles Lodge—for the most part tastefully done. The road will now be busy and getting busier as you approach the coast. If you don't mind that, you can proceed, intersect with Highway 1, and go north to the busyness of Carmel and Monterey or south into the magnificence of Big Sur.

On one of our excursions we did sneak into Carmel, mostly to visit Tor House, the coarse beach-stone home and tower built by the poet Robinson Jeffers in 1919. Though now pretty much surrounded by residential Carmel, it's still an impressive monument to Jeffers and his appreciation of the coast.

The forty miles of coast from Big Sur north to Elkhorn Slough is amazing in its diversity. Those of a literary bent can visit Henry Miller's haunts and Jeffers's tower. For butterfly watchers there are the monarch butterfly sanctuaries in Pacific Grove. For beach people, Carmel City Beach, Carmel River State Beach, and others up and down the coast. For mission aficionados, the Carmel Mission. For walkers, parks everywhere, a good one being the Garland Ranch Regional Park in the Carmel Valley. For birders, the whole region, with Elkhorn Slough perhaps the most interesting.

For those who wish to view *the* ultimate California coastal scenes, there are the rocky cliffs of Point Lobos and Big Sur. For whale-, porpoise-, and bird-watchers, boat trips on Monterey Bay. And for everyone, the Monterey Bay Aquarium and the sea otters in the kelp beds just offshore.

But if you don't have that kind of time, or aren't in a coastal mood, you can, so to speak, skip town. A couple

of miles to the west of the village of Carmel Valley, the Laureles Grade (G20) takes off to the north and, after six miles of interesting ascents and descents, intersects with Route 68, the Monterey-Salinas Highway, which takes you back to Highway 101.

## SOME PLACES WE LIKE

✘ Keefer's Restaurant and motel; just west of the Canal Street exit off Highway 101 in King City; (831) 385-4843.

✘ Quail Lodge; 8205 Valley Greens Drive, Carmel; (831) 624-2888.

✘ Bernardus Lodge and Marinus Restaurant; 415 Carmel Valley Road, Carmel; (831) 659-3131.

✘ Chateau Julien Winery; 8940 Carmel Valley Road, Carmel; (831) 624-2600.

✘ Los Laureles Lodge; 313 West Carmel Valley Road, Carmel Valley; (831) 659-2233.

✘ Tor House; P.O. Box 2713, Carmel, CA 93921; (831) 624-1813.

✘ Monarch butterfly sanctuaries; Pacific Grove; (831) 373-3304.

*Tor House still overlooks the sea at Carmel. The Robinson Jeffers property is somewhat squeezed in on all sides by houses. Once it was clean and open to the sea. The air is crisp here, just off the coastal shore.*

*Chapter Ten*

## PALO ALTO TO PESCADERO

*A 40-mile drive
from civilization to
the sea—less than
half a day.*

# PALO ALTO TO PESCADERO

One of the San Francisco Bay Area's most appealing features is the proximity of its open spaces to its ever burgeoning population. There are places everywhere where one can, with little effort, envelop one's self in solitude, only a few miles from seven million people. There are thousands of acres of golden rolling hills, beaches, forests, marshes, redwoods, hills, parks, and trails. There are places within sight of the towers of the Golden Gate Bridge where mountain lions and bears prowl up high, and otters fish and frolic down below.

*View of Pescadero farm just east of the town proper.*
*Hundreds of goats in the pasture. Dogs bark at me for a*
*long time. Motorcyclists roar past behind me at great*
*speed on Pescadero Road.*

South from San Francisco, Highway 1 follows the coast. It's a great road, and always interesting, but because of the increasingly hilly terrain and the cost of maintaining roads through the winter storm season, there aren't many roads connecting it to the major bay-side cities. But when one does drive into those hills, it's difficult to believe there's a major metropolitan area anywhere in the neighborhood.

This short route—covering twenty miles as the crow flies, but closer to forty on the roads—offers a bit of everything: at one end, the bay and upscale suburbs of San Francisco; and along the way, an interesting mix of Northern California mountains, creeks, redwoods, marshes, and coastal scenes.

We started at the popular Palo Alto Baylands Nature Preserve. Though not vast, the preserve, with its Lucy Evans Baylands Nature Interpretive Center, duck pond, tidal mudflats, walkways, and such, is a great example of how valuable a properly restored bay wetland can be to a community.

You enter and leave the preserve on Embarcadero Road, which interchanges with Highway 101. On leaving, the best choice is to stay

on Embarcadero for a while. It goes through downtown Palo Alto (with its shopping, bookstores, restaurants, and the like) and affords a quick look at the sophisticated environs of Stanford University. After passing through town you can turn left, to the south, on either Alma Street or El Camino Real, go down to the Oregon Expressway, and turn right.

The rate of change as one moves from the flats, up the Oregon Expressway, and then onto Page Mill Road, is quite amazing. Despite the continuing development and increasing population by the bay, and the intrusion into the hills of some mega-mansions, there has been little change up high—and less with every mile.

Crossing the ever present San Andreas Fault, Page Mill Road ascends the east slope of the hills to Skyline Boulevard, the remarkable ridge road that starts as a one-lane track down near Los Gatos and runs nearly forty miles northwest to the environs of San Francisco. At the Skyline intersection, Page Mill becomes Alpine Road. You are now facing the wetter, thickly forested west slope of the Santa Cruz Mountains, and Alpine Road dives right into it. At times it's so primeval that the civilization left behind is soon forgotten, in part because the road demands one's continual attention. The surface is decent enough but it's narrow, and its ups and downs and wiggly curves don't allow much time for sightseeing. There aren't many places to stop, but every once in a while the road emerges from the darkness onto a blazing-bright meadow with views out over the Pacific. There is, thankfully, very little traffic, and along certain stretches, the Steller's jays—if their screeching is any indication—clearly assume the woods belong to them.

There *are* indications of civilization: parks, trails, horse crossings, occasional vineyards, and Christmas tree farms, but not enough to alter the impression of being in a wilderness. Even for those of us acquainted with the territory, it takes a while to appreciate the vast nature of these west-facing slopes.

After about three miles, Alpine bends to the right at an intersection, and after an additional four miles or so comes to another intersection. Here our route turns left onto Pescadero Road, which wends its way through redwoods and creek-side gulches in descending to the flats. As the forest gives way, the scene becomes coastal. There are pastures, old houses, and small farms. No grand-scale agribusiness here, just some nurseries and lush green plots of vegetables and strawberries—and the clear impression of a different pace down here than on the other side of the mountain.

In the midst of the greenery, about four miles from the coast, is the Phipps Ranch. This fruit, vegetable, and berry farm—with educational activities for kids, meandering trails through its fifty acres, and farm animals—is sort of an all-purpose family farm. And if you happen to be into dried beans, with over one hundred varieties they're sure to have what you're looking for.

The town of Pescadero is three miles short of the sea. Most of the time it's a typical old "sleepy coastal village," but on weekends the action picks up. There aren't many other towns in the neighborhood, and certainly no other Duarte's Tavern. Housed in a drab old wooden building, Duarte's has been around since 1894, cranking out burgers and beer in addition to its crab sandwiches and famed artichoke soup. It's not haute cuisine, but it's hearty and popular. Weekend crowds can, on occasion, approach standing-room-only proportions, but the staff is fast, the crowd friendly, and the scene laid-back and fun.

The proper place to conclude this route is at Pescadero State Beach, just above the Pescadero Road intersection with Highway 1. Three parking areas are strung out along the west side of the highway, with short trails to the rocky shore, picnic tables with great views, and a good selection of birds out on the rocks.

This would be a good place to reflect upon the remarkable extent to which much of the territory you have just traveled has been protected. In the course of this forty-mile run, Page Mill, Alpine, and Pescadero Roads have passed through the Los Trancos, Monte Bello, Skyline Ridge, and Russian Ridge Open Space Preserves; Portola Redwoods State Park; Heritage Grove, Sam MacDonald, and Pescadero Creek County Parks; San Mateo County Memorial Park; Pescadero Marsh Natural Preserve; and Pescadero State Beach. Between San Francisco and Santa Cruz, the number of parks, preserves, and beaches approaches fifty.

Before departing, there's one more place to spend some time. The Pescadero Marsh Natural Preserve is just across Highway 1 from the state beach. The best way to get there is to walk from the middle parking lot (with the large sign reading "Pescadero State Beach and Natural Preserve"). You can also access the marsh from Pescadero Road via a pull-out and trailhead on the north side of the road just before the Highway 1 intersection. The trail that meanders through the marsh is interesting and offers some of the best birding in the region. Every once in a while a rare migrant hunkers down for the winter and attracts birders from all over the Bay Area.

## OTHER ROUTES TO TRY

✘ If you have no interest in the Baylands Nature Preserve in Palo Alto or the traffic in the area, you can pick up Page Mill Road from Interstate 280, or you could start in the south (say, in Los Gatos or Saratoga) and go up Skyline Boulevard to the intersection of Page Mill and Alpine Roads.

✘ For an adventurous return trip, a somewhat lengthy and wiggly route would be to head south from the Pescadero Road/Highway 1 intersection for about twenty-five miles to Davenport and then turn into the hills on Bonny Doon Road. There's a maze of mountain roads up there, but after thirty miles or so you can't help but end up on Route 9. It will then intersect with Skyline Boulevard only six miles south of the Alpine Road intersection where you started your descent to Pescadero.

✘ The coastal run along Highway 1 south from Pescadero passes a number of interesting places:

The classic Pigeon Point Lighthouse, just a few miles to the south of the intersection, can be toured on weekends. It's also a hostel, open to all ages, as are a number of other lighthouses along the coast. (For tour reservations, call (650) 879-2120; for information about the hostel, call (650) 879-0633.)

The Ano Nuevo State Preserve, home to a large colony of elephant seals, is a few miles south of the lighthouse. Elephant seals are huge, rather gross creatures that attract large crowds during the breeding season, and are worth seeing—maybe once. I've always found the birding and people-watching on the preserve more interesting than these creatures. Tours of the colony are regulated and frequently booked far in advance; call (650) 879-0227.

The village of Davenport, on Highway 1 about twenty-five miles south of the Pescadero Road intersection, is a pleasant place, with a couple of interesting shops and eateries. It's also home to U.S. Abalone, better known as U.S. Abs, a recent addition to the burgeoning West Coast aquaculture scene. As natural supplies of salmon, trout, mussels, and oysters are being depleted, more are being grown on coastal farms. Trying to make a living growing abalone, this rarest and most sought-after coastal delicacy, has proved too unpredictable for most of those who have attempted it. But U.S. Abs may have the answer: they are producing not only abalone, but an even rarer commodity, abalone *pearls*. (Phone: (831) 457-2700)

## SOME PLACES WE LIKE

✘ Phipps Ranch; 2700 Pescadero Road;
(650) 879-0787.

✘ Duarte's Tavern; 202 Stage Road, Pescadero;
(650) 879-0464.

*Chapter Eleven*

## SAN FRANCISCO TO POINT REYES

*A short run to, and through, a magnificent national seashore.*

*About 40 miles—only a few hours.*

There is a spacious view of Drakes
Bay from Chimney Rock Observation Point just off
the road to Point Reyes Light Station. One can stay here
a long time transfixed by the all-encompassing views of the bay.

# SAN FRANCISCO TO POINT REYES

Of a number of roads in Marin County that offer an
interesting mix of urban and rural, Earl and I chose Lucas Valley Road.
The Lucas Valley Road/Smith Ranch Road exit off Highway 101
is about fifteen miles north of the Golden Gate Bridge. Smith Ranch Road
and Lucas Valley Road are one and the same—Smith Ranch to the east of
101, Lucas Valley to the west. As we had never been out Smith Ranch
Road, we decided to have a look. The obvious action was centered in the
John F. McInnis County Park, with its facilities for
all manner of sporting activities.

A road around the back of the park leads to the Marin County Waste Water Facility. Such facilities are particularly attractive to birders (and, as a rule, only to birders), but this was an exception. There are dikes, grasslands, and an assortment of dirt roads that provide extensive views out to the bay. The birding's excellent, but be careful, as some of the dike roads are extremely narrow, without pull-outs. Best to walk them.

Thirty years ago Lucas Valley Road was a genuine back road and, though far from that now, it still courses through the same archetypally beautiful countryside. That Marin County is over 90 percent undeveloped is a credit to all—its local governmental agencies, environmental organizations, and a citizenry far more environmentally astute than most.

It helps, of course, that the majority of this citizenry is extremely well off, as is obvious as you set off through the valley. There are golden hills, redwoods, old and new homes, old ranches, and the ranches of the newly rich and famous.

Though it seems much longer, Lucas Valley Road runs for only twelve miles, to Nicasio Valley Road. The village of Nicasio is a mile to the north of the intersection.

Bay Area people speak of two Marins: *Marin* is what you pass through on the way to Nicasio. *West Marin* is where you are when you get there: a relatively unpopulated mix of dairies, horse country, and glorious open space—remarkably open for being so close to civilization.

Nicasio hasn't changed much over the years and is intent on remaining West Marin no matter what. Quiet most of the time, it cranks up on Saturdays and Sundays, when the weekenders cruise the territory and hunker down at the historic Rancho Nicasio for good food, drink, and live music.

*St. Mary's Church, 1867, marks Nicasio, this time of year surrounded by bright green grass and lichen-covered warm gray rocks.*

We headed north on Nicasio Valley Road, which runs along the edge of Nicasio Reservoir for three miles before terminating at the Point Reyes Petaluma Road. The route turns left here. After three more miles, a right turn over the bridge and another three miles take you into the "capital" of West Marin, Point Reyes Station.

Eternally struggling to preserve its rural character, counter the growth bug, develop affordable housing for its workers and oldsters, and survive the weekends, Point Reyes Station is surviving, and hasn't changed all that much. In truth, for us outsiders, there have been more pluses than minuses, particularly in the food department. In addition to the venerable Station House Cafe, which has served so well for so many years, there are new places, including the wonderful Tomales Bay Foods with its offerings of local produce, Marin artisanal cheeses, and other interesting items.

The town's principal distinction (some locals would, no doubt, opine *curse*) is its proximity to Point Reyes National Seashore, perhaps the Bay Area's greatest natural asset, which, in a region abounding in same, is saying something.

Point Reyes is a vast and varied peninsula projecting out into the Pacific, with trails, world-class beaches, ponds, coves, estuaries, lagoons, wildflowers, critters, picnic grounds, and vistas to satisfy the most demanding traveler.

There's even a mystery, in that the debate continues as to whether Francis Drake did, or did not, in 1579 spend three weeks repairing the *Golden Hinde* while anchored in what is now known, appropriately or not, as Drakes Bay.

The mystery was immeasurably enlivened by the 1936 discovery of a brass plaque, presumably fabricated on the *Golden Hinde,* which took, "in the name of Herr Maiesty Qveen Elizabeth of England . . . possession of this Kingdome. . . ." It was some forty years before it was, with great reluctance, deemed that the plaque was a most ingenious hoax.

However, winter storms have recently rearranged a section of the beach at Drakes Bay and opened up a cove of a shape remarkably similar to one on a map in Drake's log. This locally ballyhooed discovery has given the Drake fans of the region the current bragging rights over similar groups up and down the Pacific coast who tout *their* harbors as Drake's stopping place.

The outer reaches of the Point, north and west of Drakes Bay, are legendary in the birding community. As a West

Coast version of Cape Cod in its reach out into sea, there's an ever-lengthening list of rarities that turn up here from all over the West and Pacific Rim, particularly in the late summer and fall. When the rare-bird alarm sounds and the phone tree activates, the hotshot birders are into their cars and planes. In 1978 I happened to be over there on the morning following the arrival of North America's first Eurasian skylark, and you would've thought it was Sir Francis himself who had appeared. (The bird, utterly lackluster in behavior and appearance, then proceeded to astonish us all by returning to the same smelly cow pasture for seven consecutive years.)

And finally, there's the Point itself, with its lighthouse a steep 310 steps down the cliff, not only a scene

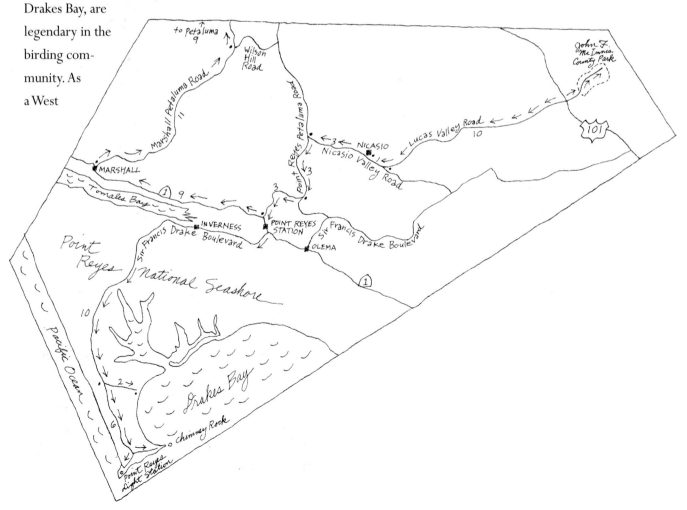

in itself but one of the best sites for seasonal whale watching on the West Coast.

For those of us who have meandered about on Point Reyes for years, the lasting impression is our regard for the visionaries who convinced the feds to protect this treasure before the developers discovered it. Fifty years ago, in order to get to the tip of Limantour Spit, you had to walk by an endless row of ugly homes; twenty-five years later, I arrived one day to find the houses *gone.* Amazing. The spit again belonged to us!

There are good roads from Highway 1 to various aspects of Point Reyes: from Point Reyes Station, through Inverness, and out to the fork that heads left to the lighthouse and right to Tomales Point; from the south, via Stinson Beach and Bolinas; and from near Olema out to Limantour. If you're new to the area, the best approach is to start at the handsome Bear Valley Visitor Center just west of Olema, where the amiable staff will provide you with maps and all you want to know.

When heading out onto the Point keep in mind that, projecting as it does into the ocean, it can have oceanic weather completely unrelated to what's happening ashore. Be prepared for anything.

## ANOTHER ROUTE TO TRY

A delightful return route to all points east can be initiated by driving back to Highway 1 and heading north along Tomales Bay for ten miles or so to the village of Marshall. Many years ago I bought a book, *Back Roads of California,* by an artist unknown to me at the time, one Earl Thollander, and in looking through it, I noticed, on a small map concerned with other places, the Marshall Petaluma Road. Running twenty miles from Marshall to Petaluma, this classic country road has been for all these years an instant cure for whatever ails me.

## SOME PLACES WE LIKE

✗ Station House Cafe; in the middle of Point Reyes Station, just off Bear Valley Road; (415) 663-1515.

✗ Tomales Bay Foods; 80 Fourth Street, Point Reyes Station; (415) 663-9335.

✗ Point Reyes National Seashore; (415) 464-5100.

*Chapter Twelve*

∿

# SANTA ROSA TO THE MOUTH OF THE RUSSIAN RIVER

*A drive through new and old Sonoma County.*

*About 30 miles—a half day.*

*The Old Town of "Georgetown."*

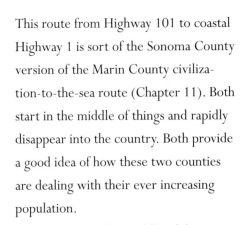

# SANTA ROSA TO THE MOUTH OF THE RUSSIAN RIVER

This route from Highway 101 to coastal Highway 1 is sort of the Sonoma County version of the Marin County civilization-to-the-sea route (Chapter 11). Both start in the middle of things and rapidly disappear into the country. Both provide a good idea of how these two counties are dealing with their ever increasing population.

We started in the middle of things in Santa Rosa. The Coddingtown Shopping Center, Sonoma County's first mega-mall, sits by the Guerneville Road exit from Highway 101. Begun in 1955, Coddingtown was a harbinger of the county's future and has transformed the intersection from the back-road turnoff to Guerneville to a multilaned and sig-naled complex.

I knew from Earl's expression and his acknowledged aversion to city life that I, the designated driver, was expected to depart this scene ASAP. At the first traffic light, heading west, we encountered a glimpse of what once we were and what we have, alas, become: in the left lane was a mottled old wreck of a VW van with the license plate BED BUS, and on the right a huge new silver SUV with dealer plates. We followed the former.

I had no idea where we were headed. Though I was acquainted with the neighborhood, native Californian Earl, in his endless search for old barns, tank houses, and other subjects, had prowled these roads far more than I. He announced that we were on our way to Georgetown. I had never heard of this Georgetown, so I shut up and followed directions.

As we drove, Earl told me that tracking down Georgetown hadn't been easy. Earl's a map man. He'd been trained in map reading in the Navy and considered himself rather expert in the field. After he heard something about Georgetown in a casual conversation, he checked all his Sonoma County maps and could find no sign of it. He started making some calls and learned, finally, what Georgetown was all about—and how to get there.

First we passed continuous rows of corporate parks and condos; then houses, mostly new, but here and there an encircled farmhouse of the past. Then a few trees flashing fall colors. That was encouraging. Farther along, fewer houses, a horse or two, some open fields, and the first of many vineyards.

About seven miles out of Santa Rosa, a left turn onto Frei Road initiated the transition into old, or at least older, California. Vineyards everywhere now, brilliantly gold. Bluebirds on grape stakes, brilliantly blue.

Georgetown, hidden away off Frei Road, is a most extraordinary happening. George Smith, a gentleman of considerable years who announced right up front that he "talks too much" ("an understatement," his wife Joyce warned us), is the creator and curator of the most unusual and colossal collection of memorabilia any of us may ever see.

George is something else. Raised in Malibu, Guadalcanal veteran, friend to the stars and jack of all trades, he has, over the past forty-five years—with his wits, good nature, and perhaps a touch of good old California cunning—created a work of folk art that, as one strolls about, takes on a life of its own. You'll find a sculpture of gnarled harnesses, a mosaic of old beer cans, a traffic jam of ancient cars—the whole place a charming, if somewhat chaotic, museum. He has so much stuff that he constructed buildings out of scrounged and gifted materials to store it. Soon there were buildings enough for an avenue and, finally, avenues enough for a village. Hence, George-town.

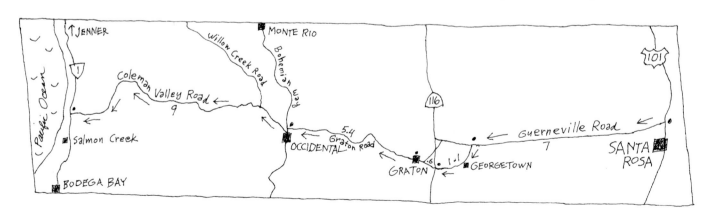

And everywhere, in this island among the vineyards, trees: a mix of redwoods and sycamores full of northern flickers, American robins, scrub jays, and lesser goldfinches escaping the monotony of the vines.

One could go on—almost as long as George does: "There's the carriage Clark Gable rode in *Gone With the Wind* . . . There's my first baseball bat . . . There's the rifle that killed three of our boys in Guadalcanal . . . Watch out for Ralph [his gimpy dog, in dog years older than he] . . . There's Louis B. Mayer's limo . . . There's Tom Mix's saddle . . . Over there, sign the guest book . . . There's the picture Ronald Reagan gave me . . . Where the hell's Earl?" (Earl has a way of dematerializing in his search for perfect perspectives.)

About all one can do is be amazed, and listen. George's conclusion: "I guess I got carried away."

Though one could spend days poking about Georgetown, there were still miles yet to go. We continued winding along Frei Road to the blinking light and went straight ahead, onto Graton (pronounced GRAY-ton) Road. On this corner, hidden away in a tractor showroom, is a new addition to the neighborhood, the Ace in the Hole Pub.

In prime apple country, the Ace in the Hole specializes in draft hard ciders made on the premises. They're tasty brews, a proper reminder that, despite the local preoccupation with the grape, there *are* other worthwhile products in this neck of the woods.

Continuing along Graton Road, within a minute or so we were into the town of Graton. While Graton *is* on the map, it has never attracted much attention. Until recently it's been a farmworkers' settlement, without much town to it, a place where you went to find day laborers looking for work.

Well, Graton's still that, but it's on a roll, and could indeed be approaching "destination" status. The north side of the main (and really only) street in town has been brought back to life by the combined efforts of a number of locals, their names on bright new bricks incorporated into the sidewalk. There are more restaurants per capita along this mini-Main Street than anywhere in the territory. The Willow Wood Market & Cafe has been around a while and is increasingly popular with locals and travelers alike. There's also a bookstore and, on the corner of Ross Road, the Blackstone tasting room featuring their Blackstone, Mark West, and Martin Ray wines.

Martin Ray in Graton? Ray, who died in 1976, was, besides being somewhat of an *enfant terrible,* a true pioneer of the post–World War II California wine industry. He turned out prizewinning wines that were often wonderful, sometimes weird, but always memorable. The original winery was atop a hill down in Saratoga, but closed many years ago. Blackstone bought the last of Ray's Saratoga wines, took over the name, and is now making Martin Ray wines—which are *still* winning prizes. Ray would be proud. (If they weren't winning prizes, he'd be haunting the place.)

There are only a few other establishments in town, with probably more to come—hopefully not too many. Graton's charm is fragile. Were it to lose track of its agricultural, Latino roots, it could become just another "quaint" California town.

If you have time for a detour of a half hour or so, turn right at the tasting room, onto Ross Road. About two miles to the north, at the T intersection, turn left onto Ross Station Road. Just a short way up the road, past the two blueberry farms (fresh berries for about six weeks, starting in June), you'll see signs to the Iron Horse Ranch & Winery. A notable small winery set on a knoll midst vineyards, olives, and palms, Iron Horse overlooks one of the great views in the wine country, with Mount St. Helena ruling the eastern horizon.

Backtrack now to Graton Road and turn right, to the west. The next few miles provide good examples of the sundry influences that altitude and exposure have in a Mediterranean climate. A sunny, southwest-facing slope will be dry and rather forbidding, while the other side of the hill will be lush, with redwoods and almost-rain forest in the shady and frequently foggy gulches. Trickles and arroyos, benign in summer and fall, become rivers, and occasionally scary torrents, during the winter rains.

After about five miles or so, Graton Road ends at a T intersection with Bohemian Highway. You're close, now, to The Bohemian Club—or, as it's known locally, for its substantial and secreting stand of redwoods, The Grove. By any name, The Grove is that unique, some might venture bizarre, three-thousand-acre all-male hangout for the rich and famous that, since moving to these parts in 1898, has been the cause of some envy and the butt of many, mostly bad, jokes. The club was founded in 1872 by a group of struggling San Francisco artists—"Bohemians"—and subsequently joined by prosperous San Franciscans interested in cavorting with artists. Eventually, there were more of the prosperous than the struggling, and the club began to evolve into what it has become. (One most definitely does *not* drop in at The Grove.)

Turn left, to the west, on Bohemian Highway and you're immediately into the town of Occidental. There have been a number of explanations for the name Occidental. Some say it was a reaction to the nine-teenth-century influx of Chinese immigrants, but in truth the name preceded the Chinese. Before there was much of a town, there was a school, established in 1864. It was called the Occidental School, for in those days the word *occident* was often used when referring to

*Georgetown, near Sebastopol.*

*The Bohemian Cafe at Occidental.*

the West or to that realm of the sky where the sun set. The town was subsequently named after the school.

The town is a charming collection of turn-of-the-century structures, two of which—the Union Hotel and Negri's—have been purveying to their loyal fans what must be the most immense family-style meals in California. Year after year. Course after course. Calorie after calorie. On my first visit to the Union Hotel, on a Sunday morning many years ago, we were sure we had finished two or three times, only to be confronted with another platter of *more*. It was an overwhelming, but not altogether unpleasant, challenge.

For the less famished, and the increasing number of those who no longer rate their meals by size, there are other options: juice bars and eateries, including Mexican. And California fare of other sorts, such as "Magical Gifts, "Elixirs," "Natural Connections," and "Positive Images." Hence, Occidental, though small and unassuming, has become a full-service town.

Earl and I were in Occidental on a November weekday and were, as best we could tell, the only outsiders in town. The locals were an intriguing mix, the younger generation sporting nose rings and purple hair, and some of the oldsters oxygen tanks and walkers. One guy had two chihuahuas sticking out of his shirt. As we were not prepared for big-time eating, we had a sandwich and a cool beer out on the pleasant porch at the Bohemian Cafe.

Coleman Valley Road commences at Jerry's service station in midtown Occidental, and as the road climbs to the west, the scene becomes increasingly coastal. In contrast with inland California, it is now green, not golden, and forested by firs and redwoods rather than oaks and madrones.

About two miles out of town, watch for a tricky turn to the right where the road drops down into Coleman Valley. Not much traffic now, and the road's so narrow there's not enough width for a center line—the true indicator of a *genuine* back road. There are, however, along its roller-coastering nine miles, plenty of pull-outs and vantage points, with views of where one's been and where one's going. For me, these overlooks are special indeed, for it was from up here, thirty years ago, that I spotted my first golden eagles. I was with some new bird-watching buddies who, in their single-minded pursuit of some tiny bird in the bushes, were paying little attention to the vast scene that encircled them. I, the recent emigré from the canyons of Manhattan, was awed by the vistas—the Coast Range, the redwoods, the Pacific—and while taking them all in, noticed, far off over a ridge, two soaring, flat-winged birds, dark and large. I suggested to my companions that they might be eagles. "Well, it is a good place for eagles," they noted, but continued to be preoccupied with the elusive nondescript. Finally, however, in response to my repeated urgings, they broke away just long enough to confirm my sighting.

There are a few houses along the road in Coleman Valley, but later on not much of anything. The ocean usually comes into view about six miles out of Occidental, but on our initial run along this route, our first view of the sea was not to be. The "sea" this day was a vast Pacific fog bank, lurking, probing the coastal grooves and gulches in preparation for its daily incursion. (And, alas, there were no eagles.)

Instead of the route's anticlimatic, and on this cool gray afternoon, lonely, intersection with Highway 1, Earl thought a better conclusion would be eight miles to the north, in Jenner, where the Russian River reaches the sea. We moved, fast as we could—never very fast on Highway 1—past a selection of Sonoma coast state beaches, each with its unique coastal outlook. After about six miles, we came to the left turn down into Goat Rock State Beach. This is the largest of these local coastal parks and offers views of the sea and its flock of rocks, the mouth of the Russian River, and Jenner across the way. We drove a couple of miles to a point where Earl could take all this in as he sketched. I went off to search the sky above the river for ospreys and the river's beach for shorebirds.

A few minutes later I scanned the hill for Earl. No Earl, just fog. When I drove back to see how things were going, he was fogged in, and out of business. (Rain and fog and leaky pens are the Darth Vaders of Earl's creative life.) So we packed up and headed home.

## ANOTHER ROUTE TO TRY

From Jenner, you have the option of an alternate route home that's a fine one in its own right, with more redwoods and water than the Coleman Valley way. From Jenner, drive east along the Russian River on Route 116, turn left onto River Road at the fork in Guerneville, and take River Road back to Highway 101 and Santa Rosa.

## SOME PLACES WE LIKE

✘ Georgetown. Unlike the other places we've visited on our routes, Georgetown is not open to drop-in traffic. Things are sort of in limbo right now, as the place—if it's to survive—is going to need continual maintenance and financial support. You can, however, call George Smith, and tell him you're going to die of curiosity if you can't come over sometime and have a look. His phone number is (707) 823-6645. Get a big group together and kick in five dollars a head, or a smaller group at ten dollars or so. If possible, go during the week, and when it's warm: George's bad leg frets in the cold.

✘ Ace in the Hole Pub; 3100 Gravenstein Highway, North Sebastopol (though it's closer to Graton); (707) 829-1223.

✖ Willow Wood Market and Cafe; 9020 Graton Road, Graton; (707) 823-0233.

✖ Blackstone and Martin Ray wine tasting room; 9060 Graton Road, Graton; (707) 824-2401; daily 11 A.M. to 5 P.M.

✖ Iron Horse wine tasting room; 9786 Ross Station Road, Sebastopol; (707) 887-1507; daily 10 A.M. to 3:30 P.M.

✖ Union Hotel, Occidental; (707) 874-3555.

✖ Negri's, Occidental; (707) 823-5301.

✖ The Bohemian Cafe is now the Cafe GIO; 3688 Bohemian Highway, Occidental; (707) 874-1640.

*The idea is to finish my drawing before fog obscures all. It is cold and windy, making it difficult to hold my drawing board in position. The gulls seem to enjoy the stiff, chilly breezes.*

*Chapter Thirteen*

Sutter Home, St. Helena

~~

# WINTERS TO THE
# MENDOCINO COAST

*A journey through four
counties to Fort Bragg.*

*About 160 miles—either
one long day or two more
leisurely days.*

*Typical of the Napa Valley—a vineyard, mountain, some trees, and a Victorian-style home from an earlier, less touristy era.*

# WINTERS TO THE MENDOCINO COAST

Route 128 is Earl's backyard, as he lives within earshot of it in the hills near Calistoga. With its run through the Napa, Knights, Alexander, Sonoma, and Anderson Valleys, its access to innumerable wineries, and its matchless collection of world-class restaurants, 128 cannot, by any stretch of the imagination, be considered a back road, but we had to include it. Despite its sophistication, there are still enough pastures and orchards, barns and tank houses, goats and horses to remind you that it is indeed a country road—so you needn't be a foodie or fancier of the grape to appreciate it. Even if there were no wineries and restaurants, Route 128 would be a joy.

Start in Winters, where the road originates at the Winters exit off Interstate 505. Setting off to the west, it's about nine miles, through almond, prune, and walnut orchards, to Monticello Dam.

In 1956, the narrow canyon (a dam builder's nirvana) where the dam now stands was the passage into the idyllic Berryessa Valley. In the 1860s the local paper, the *Napa Register,* noted that the valley was:

a land of wheat; from north to south and from east to west, through all its length and breadth does its surface echo to the rustle of the plant that is to be golden with the staff of life. For fifteen miles its surface stretches away, on an unbroken waving mass, that glistens in the sunlight, and nods and bends, and toys and wrestles and grows strong in the rustle of the waving breeze.

It's a classic story. This pristine valley, picture-book Western wheat and cattle country, with a population of

*The Nichelini Winery is perched right next
to Highway 128, a narrow winding mountain road. It's eight miles to
Napa Valley from here. Not so many tourists know of this provincial,
family-owned winery, so far from the lush vineyards of Napa.*

*In St. Helena, the winery buildings
are restored and beautified with
caring landscaping.*

Sutter Home, St. Helena

five hundred, most of them residents of the village of
Monticello, was deemed by those who know what's
best—in this case the federal Bureau of Reclamation—
perfect for damming. The decision was made and, lacking a Henry Fonda or John Wayne to save them, the
dead were disinterred, the living relocated, the land
cleared, the dam built, and Lake Berryessa created. (It
is so large that for a while, until corrected, I called it
Berry-sea.)

Gained: Flood control on Putah Creek, water for
irrigation, a vast recreational resource, great fishing,
even a new home for wintering bald eagles. Lost forever: Monticello and the Berryessa Valley. A fair trade?
Who's to say? (Occasionally, during periods of severe

drought, the ghostly skeletons of Monticello's bridges
and ranches appear from beneath the waters.)

After following the lake for a short while, 128 heads
west through some of the toughest, hilliest, hottest—
and most fire-prone—terrain in Napa County. Then,
on a sharp curve en route to Lake Hennessey, you
come to the Nichelini Winery, perched somewhat pre-
cariously on a slope in the Lower Chiles Valley.

The Nichelinis have been farming and making wine
since the 1890s, and they've been doing it without the
hoopla associated with most of the big-time operations.
When some of us novices started growing grapes, we
were hesitant to approach the heavies concerning the
problems we were facing, so we'd drive up and spend

some time with Jim Nichelini—and his zinfandel—while picking his delightful brain for always-on-the-money advice.

On one of those occasions, while celebrating the completion of the miserable task of planting a mile of deer fence around my vineyard, I noted that Jim, farther into the boonies than the rest of us, had no deer fence around his. He allowed that, well, deer were browsers and never meandered *that* far into his

vineyard: "I let 'em have the first three rows. There's plenty left for me." Jim has since gone to zinfandel heaven, but the Nichelinis are still at it. The appearance of the winery hasn't changed in a hundred years, but the inner workings have been upgraded apace with the rest of the industry. Hence, the wine's better than in the old days.

There are a few miles of curves from the winery down to Lake Hennessey and then a few more to the Silverado Trail. It's worth stopping at some of the pull-outs along the lake. Bald eagles and ospreys breed in the neighborhood and can occasionally be seen cruising the lake or perched in trees near the shore.

At the intersection of 128 and the Silverado Trail, you're suddenly in the heart of the Napa

*Where Main Street ends on the northwest side of St. Helena, this mansion overlooks the Napa Valley. Palms grow ever taller, to unimaginable heights.*

Valley. There are vineyards everywhere—indeed, you're on the Rutherford Bench, probably the best region for growing cabernet sauvignon in America (in the world, some say). Route 128 crosses the valley on the Rutherford Crossroad and turns right onto Route 29 heading north. This is the main artery up the valley, passing all manner of vineyards, wineries, and related operations—big and small, rich and famous, architecturally impressive . . . or dreadful.

It extends from Rutherford to St. Helena, the charming, now gentrified "capital of the wine country," and then to Calistoga, passing to the west of the hilltop Sterling Winery—still stunning after all these years.

Sam Brannan, early entrepreneur of the upper Napa Valley, declared that he was going to put his village, gurgling with mineral springs, on the map as the "Saratoga of California," but Sam, likely in his cups, misspoke: "It'll be the Sarafornia of Calistoga," he said (we're told). And Calistoga it is, small, delightfully Western, and still gurgling—but struggling to retain its charm and identity in the face of constant pressure from the outside world. It's a town as threatened by floods of visitors as Monticello was by the waters of Lake Berryessa.

Route 128 then heads northwest through a pass in the Mayacamas Mountains, past Mount St. Helena—at 4,343 feet, the tallest mountain in the Bay Area—and into the Knights and Alexander Valleys, two gorgeous regions that have, so far, avoided the flamboyance of their Napa neighbor. There *are* wineries along the way, but the scene is dominated by the hills and by the vineyards, whose contribution is their capacity to remain brilliantly green no matter how golden-dry their surroundings.

Progressing toward the Sonoma Valley, you pass the Jimtown Store (an upscale but still charming version of the last *really* old-fashioned store in the territory), pass Geysers Road, cross the Russian River (a kiddie creek in summer, torrential thriller during the winter rains), and drive through up-and-coming Geyserville. Just above Geyserville, Route 128 joins Highway 101, which heads north toward Cloverdale.

Amongst the numerous vineyards on both sides of 101, there's one that is different from the others. Running for a few miles along the west side of the freeway, to the north of the whitewater tower, are the vast, awesomely orderly vineyards of Gallo-Sonoma, the most striking manifestation of Gallo's successful push to become a major player at the super-premium end of the wine industry. Everything is *so* neat. The rolling hills are perfectly manicured, with each stake and vine and row so identical to its neighbor that you begin to search, unsuccessfully, for a mistake or two, to assure yourself that it's for real.

You can drive through sleepy Cloverdale or take the bypass on 101. Just to the north of town, 128 heads west.

The personality of this final section of the route, from 101 to the sea, has for years been hopelessly split. The inhabitants of the settlements along the way have always treasured their glorious countryside, their isolation, and in some cases (to put it mildly) their idiosyncrasies, while living along the only convenient road by which the San Francisco swells can reach the Mendocino coast. The opportunity for easy pickins must, at times,

be overwhelming. You'd expect hokey bars, overpriced restaurants, and T-shirt shops, but there's very little of that sort of nonsense. Route 128 pretty much minds its own business and appears as it has for decades.

The town of Boonville is in the Anderson Valley, midway between Highway 101 and the coast. That novels have not been written, and documentaries made, about Boonville is a mystery—not so much because of the town's funky appearance and offerings, but the stories to be told by, and of, its residents. Amongst other things, the locals of generations ago could converse in Boontling, a language of their own invention that allowed them to communicate among themselves to the exclusion of outsiders. *Boonters* were those fluent in Boontling, but alas, there aren't many Boonters left—and absent a last-minute renaissance of interest, Boontling will be gone with the current generation.

For most travelers, there's not enough time to delve into that, but time should be afforded to take advantage of the good food and wine of the region. There's diner

*Mount St. Helena is best seen from Knights Valley, just northwest of Napa Valley on Highway 128. Its entirety is visible, rising grandly from the valley.*

food at the Horn of Zeese (the last visible remnant of Boontling in the valley—a horn of zeese being, of course, a cup of coffee). If you breakfast there you can have some bill nunn on your pancakes, Bill Nunn having been a long-ago local who put syrup on everything. There's pub food and excellent brews at the Anderson Valley Brewery and some of the best food and lodging you'll find anywhere, at the old Boonville Hotel. And if your cell phone's not connecting (as is likely), you can use the buckey walter out on the corner—a buckey being a nickel and walter being a telephone, after Walter Levi, who owned the first phone in the valley.

As you move along toward Philo (where the locals gather at Libby's for good Mexican food) and Navarro, more vineyards. In the '70s, the champagne makers from France, when evaluating the possibilities of making American sparkling wine, looked to good apple country, for where apples thrive so do chardonnay and pinot noir, the principal ingredients of proper sparkling wine. The Anderson Valley, with

its cooling fog and ocean influence, is prime apple country, so the French were right on target. The still wines from the valley's pinot noirs and chardonnays are among the best, and the sparkling wines, particularly those of Roederer, in Philo, are the best—and worth a special journey.

As a result of that vinous progress, many of the apple orchards have, alas, lost out to the grape. Luckily, however, for those who are fond of good apples, there are some tough folks in the valley who are not only sticking with apples but planting new and unusual varieties.

Just to the west of Navarro, no more vineyards. As with most Northern California roads approaching the coast, there's too much fog, and it's too cool for grapes. The redwoods take over.

Until the most recent wine boom gained momentum in the '70s, the wine country was completely lacking in upscale, or even middle-scale, restaurants: farmers had neither the time nor money to be chasing after truffle oil and duck confit.

The only available offerings were the million-calorie meals at Jonesy's, down at the Napa airport, and the dollar martinis, malfatti, and iceberg lettuce gooped with pink dressing at The Depot, an eccentric Italian place by the tracks in downtown Napa. Malfatti is The Depot's claim to fame. It is said that many years ago, while preparing a batch of ravioli, they ran out of pasta and had no choice but to separate the leftover filling into little blobs and cook them in the buff. Voilà, malfatti. (It became a valley standby, and the locals *still* come to the back door to take pots of it home for dinner.)

About a mile and a half out of Navarro, Route 128 and the Navarro River converge and for the next ten miles run in parallel through Navarro Redwoods State Park. The first time one drives from the blazing sun into the amazing shadowy realm of a bona fide redwood grove, it becomes obvious why feelings run so high about these trees. It's another world: greener, taller, with deeper, darker shadows and brighter highlights than any "typical" forest.

However, there may have been just a modicum of truth in Ronald Reagan's 1986 comment, when he was asked about a plan to enlarge Redwoods National Park: "A tree is a tree," he said. "How many more do you have to look at?" There *is* indeed a sameness about redwood groves. But for many, the clout of the redwoods

*A slight fogginess brings a film lightly obscuring the details of Mendocino town. The eternal sound of waves upon shore vibrates in the still air. I must hurry to complete my drawing before the fog becomes more intense.*

is spiritual rather than visual. They're symbolic—of ancientness, of the outsized gianthood of Western America, of what California's all about.

As the road narrows between the trees and follows the curves of the river, take your time. The trees are impressive, but even more impressive, in a sad sort of way, are the huge stumps of the virgin trees harvested generations ago.

Route 128 terminates at Highway 1, near the mouth of the Navarro River. The coast is beautiful in either direction, but aside from the charming village of Elk there's not much happening to the south. Most of the action is along the twenty miles or so

of Highway 1 to the north, up through Fort Bragg. There are motels, inns, B&Bs, and restaurants scattered along the way, offering accommodations and fare to meet most any taste.

A few miles north of the intersection, a bridge crosses the Albion River, and the village of Albion is beneath the bridge. This scene is repeated up and down the Northwest coast. Where rivers and gulches are substantial, there are bridges up high and, down below, funky fishing villages—with their seafood restaurants, shops, and often good fishing and birding. When the gulches are smaller, and the realm of creeks rather than rivers, there are parks with picnic grounds, miles of

inland trails, and surf-bashed shores.

Some prefer the deepness of the inland forests, with their ferns and flowers and waterfalls, but Earl and I find the edge of the sea more interesting, more unpredictable. One never knows just what might turn up. There are always birds, and if you look long enough,

other creatures: California sea lions, harbor seals, even whales; or, if you're *really* lucky, a spectacular harlequin duck or two frolicking in the most turbulent of the whitest waters.

Next is the village of Little River with its inns, and after another three miles or so, the town of Mendocino. But before you get there, turn toward the sea on Brewery Gulch Drive. Drive half a mile and park by the "Public Access" sign and the gate to a small park. From there, a short trail leads out to one of the great vistas in California. You're looking across roiling Mendocino Bay at the town, with its steepled church and classic row of "Mendocino houses."

As Mendocino has for generations been a sanctuary for artists, it has some better-than-average galleries. And the town itself, with its sparkling white Victorian

buildings nearly surrounded by the sea, is, in a sense, an *objet d'art.* When Earl first came upon it some fifty years ago, Mendocino was relatively deserted, with only that row of old white buildings, plenty of open space, and probably more artists than visitors. Visually it hasn't changed that much, but it has, with its restaurants and shops and bookstores, become increasingly popular with travelers.

For solitude, continue north a bit on Highway 1. You'll quickly leave the bustle of the town. Russian Gulch State Park—a creek park, and one of California's most beautiful—is just up the road. There are long

walks up into the forested gulches and some great seaside scenes. To picnic at one of the park's strategically situated tables when the sea is up can be unforgettable, with the mist, the honking gulls, and the surf crashing into the cliffs.

About seven miles to the north, at the south end of Fort Bragg, there's a long, soaring bridge over the

Noyo River and the substantial fishing village of Noyo Harbor. Commercial fishing is still a big deal here, but over the next decade or two it's likely the harbor will evolve from its current fishery-oriented status into something more outsider-oriented. Whatever its destiny, it's very much alive, with its Coast Guard station, seafood restaurants, and all manner of seaside activity. To get down there, take North Harbor Drive, the first inland turn north of the bridge.

Fort Bragg is well along in its transition from a classically dreary lumber town to an interesting destination. There are motels, hotels, and inns, a couple of commendable bookstores, and a steam-engine Skunk Train (so named because of the stinky oil once used to fire its boilers) that runs through forests and mountains to and from Willits. The shopping's good and the eating much better than you'd expect in a town of 6,500 residents.

The Restaurant, a fixture on the main street (Highway 1), has been a source of sophisticated down-home food (if that's not an oxymoron) for years. The North Coast Brewing Company serves better-than-average pub food and prizewinning brews, and the newer Rendezvous offers extremely classy meals. But despite such upscale incursions, it's heartening to see that the town still retains its commendable blue-collar aura.

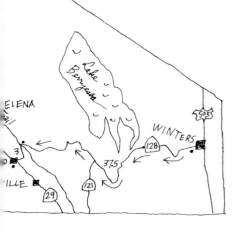

## OTHER ROUTES TO TRY

✗ When it comes time for the return trip, you could do worse than retracing your way back down Route 128. Though Earl and I abhor repeating ourselves, roads *are* different when done in reverse.

But when we were ready to head home from Fort Bragg, we consulted the local AAA about the road to Branscomb, which takes off to the east from the coast about sixteen miles north of Fort Bragg. We were in luck: the road had recently been upgraded and paved. How could we resist?

This stretch of coast is beautiful and pleasantly deserted. And if you haven't yet OD'd on state parks, MacKerricher State Park, just a few miles north of Fort Bragg, is a must. It's on the ocean side of Highway 1 and runs for *seven miles* along the coast, with tide pools, cliffs, wildflowers, black sand beaches, picnic grounds, good birding by the ocean and freshwater Lake Cleone, and as a bonus, two great wheelchair-accessible boardwalks (with passing lanes!).

About thirteen miles north of MacKerricher, just past Westport, we turned to the east on Branscomb Road, into as woodsy a setting as could be imagined. The road is excellent, but as it climbs and climbs along the knife-edge ridges leading back from the coast, it does require continual attention. The occasional views through the forest are grand indeed and have you wondering how there could be so many trees in the world. You wonder even more so when you suddenly drop down into Branscomb, a no-nonsense settlement that appears to consist essentially of one huge frenetically active sawmill, into and out of which the ex-trees roll at, depending upon your ecopolitics, an amazing or terrifying rate. Regardless, however, of whatever environmental concerns you might harbor, the place *is*

*Branscomb is active with the comings and goings of pickups, vans, and huge lumber trucks. It is big timber country, and there is a rough-and-ready feeling to this place.*

impressive—a realm where men (or at least what you can see of them through all that facial hair) are indeed still men.

We hung around Branscomb for a while. I wandered about, admiring (guiltily) the huge machines that were consuming the trees. Earl sketched the barbershop, which seemed as much a loss leader in this town as the sawmill would be in the Sahara.

We eventually pushed on to Laytonville, lunched, and headed south on Highway 101, stopping for quite a while in Hopland at an establishment that should be on every Californian's itinerary. The Real Goods Solar Living Center is a large spread; part educational institution, part museum, and part retail store that displays, designs, and sells the latest energy-saving equipment and philosophy.

*At Noyo Harbor, gulls are everywhere and noisy. They pose atop masts and ledges and posts and rails to continue their incessant squawking. Several fishing boats move seaward loaded with crab traps. Men shout from boat to shore and shore to boat.*

✗ You can also try other return routes from the coast. There's not much variety, but there are options (other than the Branscomb route): from north to south, the relatively busy Route 20 east from Fort Bragg; the Philo-Greenwood Road from Elk back to Route 128; Mountain View Road from near Manchester back to Boonville; and the extremely remote forty-mile collection of curves from Stewarts Point back to Highway 101 at Geyserville.

## SOME PLACES WE LIKE

✗ Nichelini Winery; off Route 128 at 2950 Sage Canyon Road; (707) 963-0717. As a rule the winery is open to visitors for tasting and picnicking only on the weekend, but if you call ahead, they'll try to accommodate you at other times.

✗ If one has the time and the energy, the walk up Mount St. Helena is always worthwhile and occasionally spectacular. The Silverado Mine, where Robert Louis Stevenson honeymooned in 1880, is half an hour up the trail. From the summit, the views can be awesome: on winter-clear days Lassen Peak is in the foreground and Mount Shasta looms in the distance, two hundred miles to the north. To the summit of Mount St. Helena and back—a serious workout—takes most of a day.

✗ In downtown Boonville: the Boonville Hotel (14040 Route 128, (707) 895-2210); the Horn of Zeese (14025 Route 128, (707) 895-3525); and the Anderson Valley Brewery (17700 Boonville Road, (707) 895-2353). They're all next to each other in town, on 128.

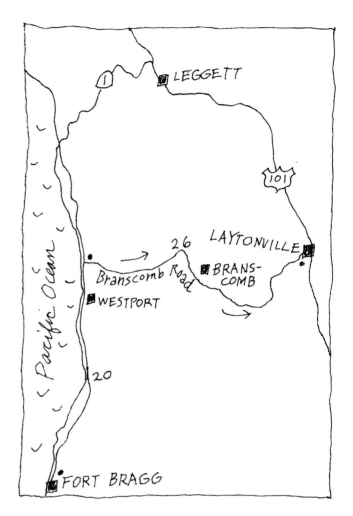

✗ Libby's restaurant; 8651 Route 128, Philo; (707) 895-2646.

✗ In Fort Bragg: The Restaurant (707-964-9800), the North Coast Brewing Company (707-964-3400), and the Rendezvous (707-964-8142) are all in town on the main street, which is Highway 1.

✗ Skunk Train; Fort Bragg; (800) 777-5865.

## Chapter Fourteen

## ALL THE WAY FROM
## NEVADA TO THE SEA

*A broad slice of
California, from the
Surprise Valley
to Eureka.*

*About 340 miles, almost
all on Route 299—two
to three days.*

*Even today, it is a surprise to come across
this green valley on the other side of
the Warner Mountains. It is pleasant and
welcoming in its silence.*

# ALL THE WAY FROM NEVADA TO THE SEA

Do this route and you'll have the opportunity to see an
extraordinary variety of what California has to offer, some of which can be found
nowhere else in the nation. Indeed, there are enough natural wonders in northeast
California to supply a nation. And as a dividend you'll be passing by, or through,
all manner of wonderful-sounding places: Hat Creek, Fort Bidwell, Whiskeytown,
Burnt Ranch, Jess Valley, Goose Lake, Skunk Point, Captain Jack's Stronghold,
Fall River Mills, Likely, Deadman's Beach, Ingot,
Surprise Valley and, of course, Eureka.

For years, Earl and I had been thinking about spending some serious time up north, but had just never gotten around to it. Now that we had the opportunity to do so, California Route 299 was the obvious answer, from its origin in Modoc County at the Nevada border to its terminus at the sea near Eureka.

Modoc County was archetypal "Indian country" and was so for longer than any other place in California. There were numerous confrontations between the Modoc, Klamath, Paiute, and Pit River Indians and the settlers traveling in wagon trains over the California-Oregon Trail, the Applegate Cutoff, and the Lassen Trail. There were killings of settlers and sundry battles between the army and the increasingly outnumbered Modocs, who fought brilliantly and bravely from the cliffs and caves of their home turf. It went on, sporadically, for years—until May 10, 1873, when the Modocs, led by Kientepoos (Captain Jack, to the Americans), launched their final attack and were, ultimately, defeated.

The nature of the landscape, the surviving traces of the Indian and pioneer cultures, the battlegrounds themselves, and most of all the historical immediacy of these struggles are quite unlike anything else in the state. There is access to it all from Route 299—and more than likely you'll be just about the only travelers in the territory.

This corner of California is classic Great Basin Range: vast, dry, and at 4,300 feet and climbing, high. At first, it looks like land only a cowboy could love (and there are some of them about, doing just that), but the more one takes it in, the more captivating it becomes. The cool and brittle air, the herds of pronghorn antelope, the raptors, the flights of winter waterfowl, and year-round crystalline creeks (from which, a colleague insists, the trout jump right into your net) make for a rare scene in a state with 34 million residents.

As far north as it is (on the same latitude as Buffalo, New York, snow capital of America) and as high as it is, Modoc County winters are for real: temperatures down to zero, snow, ice, fog, and all that. It's the only one of our routes where the weather can be a serious problem. If you head up there in winter—when it can be intriguing—be prepared, and carry chains. The same can be said for the higher sections of the road between Redding and Eureka.

Either Cedarville or Alturas is a logical place to spend a night before heading down Route 299. Both offer motels and B&Bs—nothing fancy, but adequate, with an abundance of Western hospitality. Farther along, there are plenty of places to stay and eat in Redding and, to a lesser degree, in Weaverville.

Route 299 commences on the desolate Nevada border nine miles east of quiet Cedarville. Before heading west, however, take a long look to the east, across the vast—both beautiful and forbidding—Surprise Valley, and beyond that, the Empty Quarter of Nevada. What was it like for the wagon trains that chose this route, way back when?

Drive west over Cedar Pass and down to the only city of any size in the county, Alturas. About as far from the big money as can be, Alturas, with its three thousand residents, isn't exactly thriving, but it has a fine old courthouse, the Modoc County Historical Museum and, just south of town, the small Modoc National Wildlife Refuge. The refuge has an interesting one-way dike road that meanders through its wetlands. The refuge can be reached from Route 115, which parallels Highway 395 just south of Alturas.

From Alturas, Route 299 begins its 145-mile downhill meander to Redding. Along the way it passes through one beautiful valley after another—cattle country for most of the locals, but to many of us out-siders, classic Western fishing country. Earl can never understand why I stop at the bridges over such as Hat Creek and Fall River and gaze down into the water, transfixed in my search for those ultimate big ones that I've not yet landed.

Besides being a trout fisherman's dream, these and the other creeks that meander through pastures and meadows of the region are a visual delight. It would not be impossible, say, from a bridge in the Fall River Valley, to have in the foreground laser-brilliant yellow-headed blackbirds, in the distance, herds of pronghorn, and in the background Mount Shasta to the northwest and Lassen Peak to the south. Beat that!

All California birders—birders everywhere—have wish lists of the birds that have eluded them. Mine was typical: amongst others, the diabolically elusive black

rail, the unpretentious least bittern, and the (still pend-ing) great gray owl of the higher Sierra meadows. Many years ago I was told that if I drove six miles north of Route 299 on Route 89 (the intersection is about eleven miles down the road from Fall River Mills), to McArthur-Burney Falls Memorial State Park, I could add to my life list a particularly interesting and uncom-mon bird, the mysterious black swift. For whatever reason, this swallowlike speedster chooses to live behind waterfalls, hence its residence in the park.

This is a side trip that *must* be done, for Burney Falls are the most spectacular I've ever seen. (Teddy Roosevelt called the falls the "eighth wonder of the world.") Though not as grandiose as Niagara with its roar or Yosemite with its height, Burney Falls are, in truth, more interesting. Burney Creek, often bone dry upstream, erupts, year-round, from the center of the

*The Alturas Courthouse, with its red-painted dome, is a prominent architectural feature of Modoc County's main town.*

earth just a few hundred yards above the falls and then pours (more than 200 million gallons a day) over a 130-foot cliff into the mists and sprays of an extraordinarily lush green hollow. The cliff is of such porous volcanic basalt that the water comes through as well as over the cliff. You'd think you were in Paradise. And the black swift is, in season (spring and summer), what's known to birders as a "walkup," just waiting to be seen.

The towns along this ranching stretch of Route 299, which runs from Alturas down to, say, the Shasta County park on Hat Creek just east of Route 89, aren't picturesque, but you're through them in no time. And starting about twenty or so miles east of Redding, the whole scene loses any luster for a while, the result of suburban sprawl and the huge scar left by the 65,000-acre Fountain Fire of 1992. Though the region was devastated, it's interesting to see how it looks a decade later. While not pretty, it's alive and well—and coming back.

Route 299 goes on into busy and booming Redding, joins Interstate 5, runs south for two miles, and then heads west again, into the mountains. While there were plenty of hills and even the substantial Warner Mountains to the east, these mountains to the west are the real thing, particularly through the middle half of the 150 or so miles to Eureka.

First is the climb up to Whiskeytown National Recreation Area, where the views across Whiskeytown Lake, occasionally including a bald eagle or two, are quite spectacular. Weaverville, the largest town between Redding and the sea, is some twenty miles farther along.

Once one of the most inaccessible settlements in California, Weaverville was settled by miners during the gold rush years and, despite numerous fires and the gradual decline of the mines, survived as the commercial and governmental center of the region. During its mining heyday, there was a Chinese community of some two thousand laborers, the only vestige of same being the still functioning joss house (Chinese temple)

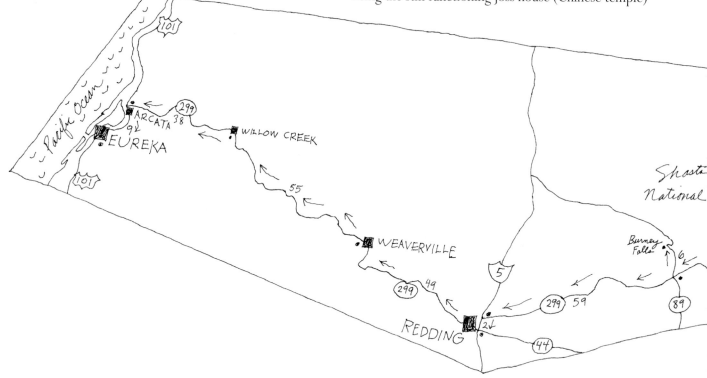

just off the main street. That, and some of the town's other old buildings, are worth some time.

Route 299 then moves into the Trinity Alps. The drive along the Trinity River, particularly when the morning sun is reflecting off its sparkling white waters, is delightful and worth doing at a leisurely pace. There are plenty of pull-outs along the way, and some riverside settlements—mostly involved in rafting or fishing—where it's possible to check out the river up close, and also score some eats.

The route leaves the mountains shortly before reaching the coast, invariably to a climate foggier and most definitely cooler than often-scorching Redding. It finally terminates at Highway 101, just a few miles north of Arcata, Eureka, and the other towns on Humboldt Bay.

Most of the action in the region is centered in Eureka, a city of thirty thousand along the east shore of the bay. Like Fort Bragg, Eureka was once a booming center of the lumber and paper industries and, like so many other cities and towns of the Northwest, fell on hard times when these industries lost their charisma. During the worst of those times, block after block of

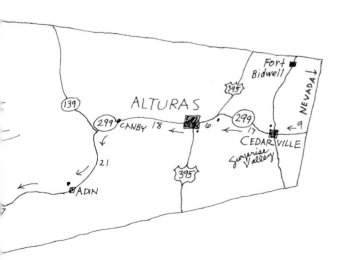

Eureka's fine old buildings seemed in danger of falling—or being knocked—down.

However, Eureka has, as they say, been pulling itself up by its bootstraps. With its neighbors, it's part of the largest coastal metropolis between San Francisco and the Portland–Seattle metropolitan complex, and in this age of travel and tourism, it's been taking advantage of that accident of geography. Every time we've been up there of late, there's more: better places to stay and eat, interesting shops, antiquarian bookstores, and some of the best birding on the West Coast.

In addition to many fine old multistory buildings in its designated (and well signed) Old Town, Eureka has some of California's finest Victorian structures. The wildly decorative Carson Mansion at M and Second Streets may be the best-known building of its sort in the nation, and its neighbors are commendable supporting players.

If you're into serious eating and wining, the elegant Restaurant 301 in the Carson Hotel is a class act, but there's a complete spectrum of restaurants—upscale and basic, ethnic and American, pricey and not—at your disposal.

Arcata, seven miles north of Eureka, is a quiet version of Eureka, with an interesting town square and its own collection of Victorians, less grandiose than Eureka's but more representative of what one sees up and down the coast.

Arcata's principal claim to fame, particularly for the environmental community, is the Arcata Marsh and Wildlife Sanctuary. Not only is the sanctuary, with its many trails, a fine place to walk, bird, and just hang out, it's also a paradigm of what can be done when concerned citizens and responsible officialdom work together in the interest of the greatest good.

In 1949, primary unchlorinated effluent from the

city of Arcata was being dumped directly into the bay. Over the years, as that practice was being terminated and the sewage system upgraded, oxidation ponds were constructed adjacent to the city's wastewater plant. As time passed, it became obvious that the environment and public works not only could coexist, but could also improve each other's lot. With the addition of more ponds, the area began to attract a remarkable spectrum of birdlife and, in 1981, with the assistance of the Coastal Conservancy, the Arcata Marsh and Wildlife Sanctuary was established. The preserve, which encompasses 154 acres and includes the Arcata Marsh Interpretive Center, has become a national model of intelligent ecology.

The center is worth visiting, as much for the getting there as for itself. It is most definitely *not* in a national park—it's just south of town in industrial Arcata, adjacent to numerous commercial operations, low-cost housing, the Culligan Man, junkyards, Roto-Rooter, and of course, the wastewater treatment plant. But it's full of birds, easily observed. To get to the center from Route 255, the main road through Arcata, go south on G Street.

There are also days and days of birding to be had in the numerous venues of the Humboldt Bay National Wildlife Sanctuary. The sanctuary's new interpretive center is along the east shore of the south bay, and is accessed just off the Hookton Road exit from Highway 101, eight miles south of Eureka.

The citizenry in general is very protective of the wildlife abounding on and near the contiguous Humboldt and Arcata Bays, and has been supported in its efforts by the faculty and students of the College of the Redwoods in Eureka and Humboldt State University in Arcata. Perhaps most indicative of the significant changes in the Humboldt Bay gestalt of late was an observation made by an Arcata walker we met on a sanctuary trail. This walker noted that whereas in past years the hardware being carted about on the shoulders of the locals would have been shotguns, these days it's spotting scopes.

*Gold Rush Coffee in Eureka.*

## OTHER ROUTES TO TRY

✖ After you reach Arcata and Eureka on Route 299, what next? We think the next best thing is to head down to Ferndale and on to the Lost Coast (see Chapter 15). Eventually you'll end up on Highway 101 with plenty of options from there. There are, however, other interesting roads back into the northern interior. Route 36 runs from just below Fortuna down to Red Bluff. And Route 96, which splits from Route 299 at Willow Creek, heads northeast along the most remote stretches of the Klamath River and eventually intersects with Interstate 5 a half hour or so south of Ashland, Oregon. Ashland's always worth a long detour.

✖ While you're up in that far northeast corner of the state, before setting off on this route, try to fit in a run up to Fort Bidwell. It would be a shame to be this close and not drive the fifty miles round trip from Cedarville to Fort Bidwell, *the* last outpost in California. Huddled up against the Warner Mountains on the west edge of the Surprise Valley, Fort B's clapboard homes and cool creeks seem more like New England than California. Far from everywhere, the small town hasn't much of an economic base. The old general store is iron-doored shut, and the town's only mansion, next door, is showing its considerable age. However, retirees are arriving, looking for escape from the ever escalating pace of the rest of California. Having to drive twenty-five miles and back for a quart of milk is a small price to pay.

Many years ago, on our first visit to Fort Bidwell, we were amazed to encounter a chic couple from Los Angeles who had bought the mansion and were planning to convert it into a hotel-restaurant. They had been driving over by Goose Lake (on the west side of the Warners), saw the sign to Fandango Pass (how could anyone resist that name?), came over the mountain into Fort B—and resolved never to leave. There was no question that the mansion was perfect for a hotel-restaurant—except that nobody ever comes to Fort Bidwell. They gave it their best, but it wasn't too long before reality set in.

The unpaved Fandango Pass Road heads off to the west about five miles south of Fort Bidwell and runs over to one of California's greatest north-south roads, Highway 395. There are a number of stories as to the origin of the name of the pass, at 6,100 feet the last great hurdle for the wagon trains heading into Northern California. Legend has it that in the early 1850s a group of immigrants, celebrating their successful crossing of the pass, were dancing the fandango when they were dispatched by the local natives.

## SOME PLACES WE LIKE

✖ Restaurant 301; 301 L Street, Eureka; (707) 444-8062.

✖ Humboldt Bay birding information, (707) 826-7031.

*Chapter Fifteen*

## EUREKA TO
## GARBERVILLE

*A stretch of genuine
back roads along
California's Lost Coast.*

*A drive of 100
miles—half a day
to a whole day.*

*The aptly named gumdrop trees of Ferndale are one of the sights of this coastal town.*

~ ~

There's one more route that *must* be done: the Lost Coast. It's short,
but slow paced, and quite unlike our other routes. It's not as much a
road *to* the seacoast as a road *beside* the sea.
Highway 1, Highway 101, and to a lesser extent Interstate
5 cover the full length of the California coast—except for the bump that extends
out into the Pacific between Eureka and Leggett. Most of this region is so remote
that the road builders directed Highway 101 away from it and, at
Leggett, simply decided to give up on Highway 1 altogether.

It's called the Lost Coast because it is, for the most part, unpopulated wilderness, particularly its southern reaches. The heart of it is wild and indeed "lost" to us ordinary mortals, as the only way to appreciate it is to approach it by shank's mare with plenty of time on your hands and a pack on your back. Hence, it's beyond the purview of this book.

But it's not nearly as lost as I had imagined. There *are* roads (for the most part quite decent), and if you have the time and patience you can acquire a sense of it by taking the meandering route that runs from Ferndale to Petrolia, Honeydew, Ettersburg, Redway, and Garberville.

If you're going in winter, check with the Highway Patrol or Caltrans on road conditions. Our first trip, a few days after some February storms, was a learning experience. We had assumed that, being coastal and jutting as it does out into the Pacific, the region would be immune to winter. We were mistaken. It should have occurred to us that the principal reason for the absence of major thoroughfares was the ruggedness and altitude of much of the terrain. There was snow in abundance, on some of the roads and atop all the hills and mountains—a number of which approach four thousand feet in height.

We encountered the dreaded CARRY CHAINS, and worse, CHAINS REQUIRED signs at the base of a few grades, but the weather had moderated just enough that they weren't necessary (which was just as well, because they were in the garage back in Napa: I didn't move from the East Coast to Lotus Land to be messing around with chains). So, all things considered, the snowy scenes were more spectacular than troublesome, and enhanced the whole experience.

From Eureka, the route heads down Highway 101 for fifteen miles and exits onto Route 211. (However, more than most of our routes, the Lost Coast is enjoyable and revealing in either direction. Instead of traveling south from Eureka, you could head north from Garberville or Redway.) After crossing the fertile Eel River Delta, you arrive in Ferndale, a pleasant and civilized town that offers no clues as to the realm that lies beyond.

Ferndale, though larger than Earl and I remembered it (no doubt because it is), has retained its genuine appeal. It is California's most "Victorian" town and has conscientiously worked at preserving its treasury of Victorian architecture—without getting silly about it. It's definitely worth some time, including a stroll along Main Street and, perhaps, a visit to the charming Ferndale Museum.

*It is a surprise when this short stretch of road appears along the shore of the Pacific. It is a lonely, haunting road.*

It's not obvious, but Ferndale's dramatic setting, nestled at the base of Wildcat Ridge, is on shaky ground. The whole region is extremely unstable as a result of the Mendocino triple junction, the grinding together of the Gorda, North American, and Pacific tectonic plates just a few miles off nearby Cape Mendocino. It's the most active seismic region in the continental United States—far more so than that to the south, where the San Andreas Fault does *its* grinding.

On April 25–26, 1992, something let loose off the cape and rendered a near-fatal blow to Ferndale. Within the space of thirty hours there were *three* quakes—registering 7.1, 6.6, and 6.7 on the Richter scale. Had the town not been constructed of wood, it would have been flattened. (The beaches just up the road were hefted from one to four feet.) The recovery and rebuilding took years, but everything's back to normal. You'd never know it happened, but I guess if you lived there, you surely wouldn't have forgotten.

Ferndale's the last significant action for a while, so make sure you have gas in the tank and a plan for lunch (or dinner). The route now goes up Main Street, turns right on Ocean Avenue, and then turns left at the next corner, where there's a big old metal sign: "Capetown Petrolia." This is Mattole Road. It heads up Wildcat Ridge and into the boonies, winding about, with vistas of meadows up close, mountains to the east, and the Pacific to the west. It eventually descends and runs along five miles of the westernmost beach in California—also the most deserted California beach you'll ever see. This is what the Lost Coast is all about. In a half hour of walking about, sketching, birding, and flower watching, we crossed paths with only one car—and one cow. It's a rare scene.

The road then moves back from the coast, through the bucolic Mattole Valley and into Petrolia, the largest of the few villages in the region. There's a store, a fire station, an attractive Catholic chapel and, the day we were there, a young woman selling pizza from the back of her pickup.

There's also a plaque near the store with the news that in the 1860s some primitive wells just down the road produced California's first oil. Hence the name Petrolia. The plaque did not explain what had ever possessed anybody, way out here on the state's westernmost point, to even *think* about drilling for oil.

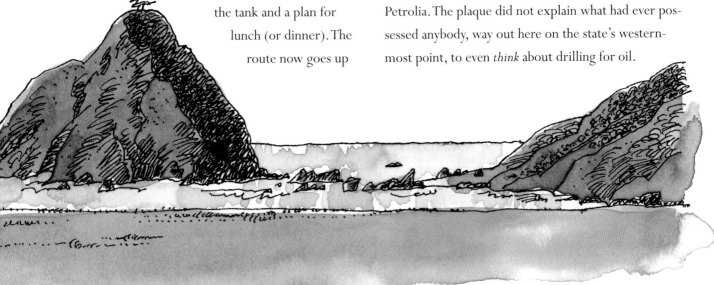

*The chapel at Petrolia.*

Mattole Road meanders on—through meadows and forest corridors, up and down hills, and around curves—into Honeydew. The route then continues, as Wilder Ridge Road, to Ettersburg, a pastoral crossroads settlement that would be a perfect setting for a Western movie. From Ettersburg—now as the Ettersburg Honeydew Road—it runs along Telegraph Ridge and, after six miles, drops down to the road that runs west to Shelter Cove and east into Redway. It's an easy run of thirteen miles into Redway, which will seem like quite a metropolis after where you've been.

In Redway, we dined at the Brass Rail. It's one of those old, woody, sort of Germanic places. (Earl and I classify restaurants as Germanic when they're dark and have at least one large stuffed animal head hanging somewhere, usually over an oversized stone fireplace.) The building's been around since 1922, has a colorful history, and under the current ownership does a pretty good job with its food and wine.

It's only a few miles from Redway to Garberville. Long famed as a hardboiled, Wild West, lumber-cutter's enclave, Garberville has changed. The locals and environmentalists are learning to live with one another. The old-timers are even beginning to see us auslanders as sources of revenue rather than tree-hugging intruders. Time will tell.

If you wish to finish this route in truly grand fashion, you could dine, and even stay, just a few miles south of Garberville at the Benbow Inn. Nestled in a forest overlooking the Eel River, the 75-year-old inn looks more Lake Country England than north-country California (even down to the English tea and scones served every afternoon), and is the sort of place where friends and families return year after year. Any

Californian who has driven north on 101 has seen it many times and has said each time: "Someday we're going to go in there and have a meal." It would be a great place to celebrate the great roads. It was for us.

## OTHER ROUTES TO TRY

The Lost Coast includes some worthy diversions from the basic route. To what degree you choose any of them will depend upon your schedule, your curiosity, and in one case, your willingness to rough it.

✗ A turn to the west where Ettersburg Honeydew Road intersects with the main road between Redway and Shelter Cove sends you, rather than east toward Redway, on a hilly run out to Shelter Cove. Shelter Cove is, in truth, not the least bit "lost." It has been found, by developers and real estate vendors who are turning it into quite a happening: big houses (why so

big?), a couple of basic eateries and places to stay and, would you believe, an airstrip. You can see why. The setting is spectacular. It may not be the sort of place some of us would choose to live, but it certainly has become so for others.

✗ For the bold—those with four-wheel-drive vehicles—there's a route through the *real* backwoods. Two miles west of that intersection where Ettersburg Honeydew Road meets the Shelter Cove road, there's a left turn that goes down through Whitethorn and almost to the coast before terminating at a four-corners choice of dirt roads. The rightmost of these, USAL Road—which becomes Chemise Mountain Road—runs up to Shelter Cove. This road is a basic, narrow, bumpy, potholed track. It's for the adventurous,

*The Benbow Inn appears at a bend in the highway surrounded by greenery, a welcome hostelry reflecting by-gone days and past pleasures. And it's still there to be enjoyed in the present.*

but it might be considered for a number of reasons. There will be grand high vistas overlooking the strikingly blue Pacific, interesting glimpses of the extremes to which some people will go for a bit of privacy, and a pass by what must be one of the most isolated educational institutions in America, the Whale Gulch School. (Read the notes on the nearby mailbox bulletin board for a notion of the neighborhood.)

✘ The other principal option is the road through Rockefeller Forest in Humboldt Redwoods State Park. This is the stretch of Mattole Road that runs east from Honeydew and intersects with Highway 101, about forty miles south of Eureka. This section of the park encompasses a huge forest of giant virgin redwoods. You would think there'd be crowds of gawkers along this meandering route so accessible from 101, but when we drove it (admittedly on a winter weekday) it was deserted, not only of traffic but of facilities. We expected gates and fees and visitor centers, but there was nothing—only the two of us and all those trees.

## SOME PLACES WE LIKE

✘ Ferndale Museum; Third and Shaw Streets, Ferndale; (707) 786-4466; walking tour maps are available.

✘ Brass Rail; 3188 Redwood Drive, Redway; (707) 923-3188.

✘ Benbow Inn; Benbow exit off Highway 101 south of Garberville; (800) 355-3301.

# Index

## A–B

Ace in the Hole Pub, 125, 130
Albion, 143, 144
Alexander Valley, 139
Alturas, 154
Alturas Courthouse, 155
Anderson Valley, 140, 141
Anderson Valley Brewery, 141, 149
Año Nuevo State Preserve, 110
Antelope Valley, 34
Antelope Valley California Poppy State Reserve, 34, 39
Anza-Borrego, 19, 21; Anza-Borrego Desert State Park, 19, 27; Anza-Borrego Visitors Center, 16
Arcata, 157
Arcata Marsh and Wildlife Sanctuary, 157, 158
Ashland, 159
Atascadero, 72
Avila Beach, 72, 73
Bakersfield, 69, 70
Banner, 21
Bart's Corner, 37, 39
Bear Valley Visitors Center, 119
Benbow Inn, 167, 169
Bernardus Lodge, 101, 103
Berryessa Valley, 136, 137
Big Sur, 101
Birding: Albion, 143, 144; Año Nuevo State Preserve, 110; Arcata Marsh and Wildlife Sanctuary, 157, 158; Coast Range, 130; Coleman Valley, 129; Elkhorn Slough, 101; Eureka, 152, 157; Humboldt Bay birding information, 159; Lake Cleone, 145; Marin County Waste Water Facility, 116; McArthur Burney Falls Memorial State Park, 155; Monterey Bay, 101; Morro Bay, 72; Mount Pinos, 35; Pescadero Marsh Natural Preserve, 109; Point Reyes, 117; Sespe Condor Sanctuary, 36; Sierra de Salinas, 100
Blackstone Winery, 125, 130
Bohemian Café, 128, 129, 130
Bohemian Club, The (The Grove), 126
Bohemian Highway, 126
Bolinas, 119
Boonville, 140
Boonville Hotel, 141, 149
Borrego Badlands, 16, 19
Borrego Springs, 16, 19
Branscomb, 145, 146, 147
Brass Rail, 167, 169
Buellton, 46
Burney Creek, 155
Burney Falls, 155
Burnt Ranch, 152
Butterflies: Monarch butterfly sanctuaries, 103; Pacific Grove, 101
Buttonwillow, 70
Byron Winery, 45

## C–E

California Missions Foundation, The, 95
Calipatria, 26
Calistoga, 139
Cambria, 82–83
Cambria Winery, 45

Captain Jack's Stronghold, 152
Carmel, 101; Carmel City Beach, 101; Carmel Mission, 101; Carmel River State Beach, 101; Carmel Valley, 98, 101–103; Carmel Valley Road, 103
Carpinteria, 39
Carpinteria State Beach, 39
Carrizo Plain, 70, 72
Carson Hotel, 157
Casmalia, 60
Cedarville, 154
Chapel of San Ramon, 42, 45
Chateau Julien Winery, 101, 103
Chimney Rock Observation Point, 114
Chocolate Mountains, 26
Cholame, 79; Cholame's Café, 79; Cholame Valley, 81; Cholame Valley Road, 79
City Café, 89, 92, 95
Cleveland National Forest, 22
Cloverdale, 139, 140
Club Fed, 63
Coast Range, 130
Coddingtown, 123
Coleman Valley, 129
Cuyama, 47
Davenport, 110
Deadman's Beach, 152
Deer Lodge, 37, 39
Depot, The, 142
Drakes Bay, 114, 117, 118
Duarte's Tavern, 109, 111
Eberle Winery, 79
Eel River, 167
Eel River Delta, 164
El Camino Real, 108
El Toreo, 33, 39
Elephant seals, 110
Elizabeth Lake Road (Route N2), 34
Elkhorn Slough, 101
Ettersburg, 164, 167
Eureka, 152, 157, 158

## F–G

Fall River, 155
Fall River Mills, 152
Fandango Pass, 159
Ferndale, 164
Ferndale Museum, 164, 169
Fort Bidwell, 152, 159
Fort Bragg, 145
Fort Hunter Liggett Military Reservation, 90
Fortuna, 159
Foxen Canyon, 45; Foxen Canyon Road, 45; Foxen Canyon Wine Trail, 49; Foxen Winery, 45
Frazier Park, 35
G20 (Laureles Grade), 103
Gallo-Sonoma Vineyards, 140
Garberville, 164, 167
Garland Ranch Regional Park, 101
Georgetown, 122, 124, 125, 127, 130
Geyserville, 139
Goat Rock State Beach, 130
Gold Rush Coffee, 158

Goose Lake, 153, 159
Gorman, 34, 35
Graton, 125
Greenfield, 98, 100
Grove, The (The Bohemian Club), 126
Guadalupe, 53
Guadalupe Nipoma Dunes Preserve, 53, 55
Guy L. Goodwin Education Center, 71, 73

## H-L

Hacienda, The, 95
Hat Creek, 152, 155, 156
Hearst Castle, 83
Heritage Grove, 109
Highways: Highway 1, 63, 83, 89, 115, 119, 149, 163; Highway 101, 72, 73, 82, 89, 91, 130, 158, 163; Highway 395, 154
Honeydew, 164, 167
Hopland, 148
Horn of Zeese, 149
Hotels. *See* Lodgings
Hughes Lake, 34
Humboldt Bay, 157; Humboldt Bay birding information, 159
Humboldt Redwoods State Park, 169
Indio, 16, 18
Interstate 5, 35, 79
Interstate 505, 136
Iron Horse Ranch and Winery, 125, 130
Jalama Beach County Park, 63
Jenner, 130
Jess Valley, 152
Jimtown Store, 139
John F. McInnis County Park, 115
Jolon, 95
Jonesy's, 142
Julian, 20, 21
Julian Grille, 21, 27
Kettleman City, 79
King City, 89, 90, 91
Kingsburg, 77
Klamath River, 159
Knights Valley, 139, 140
Lake Berryessa, 137
Lake Cachuma, 47, 48
Lake Casitas, 39
Lake Cleone, 145
Lake Hennessey, 137, 138
Lassen Park, 149
Laureles Grade (G20), 103
Laytonville, 148
Leggett, 163
Libby's, 141, 149
Limantour, 119
Little River, 144
Lockwood Valley Road, 35, 36
Lodgings: Benbow Inn, 167, 169; Bernardus Lodge, 101, 103; Boonville Hotel, 141, 149; Carson Hotel, 157; Hacienda, The, 95; Los Laureles Lodge, 101, 103; Lucia Lodge, 94, 95; Madonna Inn, 73; Parkfield Inn, 81; Paso Robles Inn, 82; Quail Lodge, 101, 103; Santa Maria Inn, 55
Lompoc, 63
Los Gatos, 108
Los Laureles Lodge, 101, 103
Los Olivos, 46
Los Padres National Forest, 35
Los Trancos, 109
Lost Coast, 159, 163, 164
Lower Chiles Valley, 137
Lucas Valley Road, 115, 116
Lucia, 94
Lucia Lodge, 94, 95
Lucy Evans Baylands Nature Interpretive Center, 108

## M-O

MacKerricher State Park, 145
Madonna Inn, 73
Maricopa Highway, 39
Marinus Restaurant, 101, 103
Mark West Winery, 125, 130

Martin Ray Winery, 125, 130
Massimi's Ristorante, 46, 49
Mattei's Tavern, 47, 49
Mattole Valley, 165
Mayacamas Mountains, 139
McArthur Burney Falls Memorial State Park, 155
McKittrick, 70
Mendocino, 144
Meridian Winery, 79
Missions: California Missions Foundation, The, 95; Carmel Mission, 101; Mission La Purisima Concepción, 61, 63; Mission San Antonio De Padua, 25, 88, 90; Mission San Antonio De Pala, 23, 25; Mission San Juan Capistrano, 31; Mission San Miguel Arcàngel, 81; Mission Santa Inés, 46; Santa Barbara Mission, 48, 49
Modoc County Historical Museum, 154
Modoc National Wildlife Refuge, 154
Montana de Oro State Park, 73
Montecito, 39
Motels. *See* Lodgings
Monterey, 101; Monterey Bay, 101; Monterey Bay Aquarium, 101
Monterey-Salinas Highway, 103
Monticello, 137
Monticello Dam, 136
Moonstone Beach, 83
Morro Bay, 72; Morro Rock, 72; Morro Strand State Beach, 72
Mount Pinos, 35
Mount Shasta, 149
Mount St. Helena, 139, 140, 149
Nacimiento-Fergusson Road, 90, 94
Napa Valley, 134, 137
Navarro, 141; Navarro Redwoods State Park, 142; Navarro River, 142, 143
Negri's, 129, 130
Nicasio, 116
Nicasio Reservoir, 117
Nichelini Winery, 136, 137, 149
Nipomo, 52
North Coast Brewing Company, 145, 149
Noyo Harbor, 145, 148
Noyo River, 145
Occidental, 126, 129
Oceano State Beach, 73
Oceanside, 25, 26
Ojai, 36, 37
Olema, 119

## P-R

Pala Indian Reservation, 23, 25
Palmdale, 31, 34
Palo Alto, 108
Palo Alto Baylands Nature Preserve, 108
Palomer, 22
Palomer Observatory, 22, 25, 27
Parkfield, 81; Parkfield Café, 81; Parkfield Coalinga Road, 81; Parkfield Grade, 81; Parkfield Park, 81
Parks/Preserves: Año Nuevo State Preserve, 110; Antelope Valley California Poppy State Reserve, 34, 39; Anza-Borrego Desert State Park, 19, 27; Arcata Marsh and Wildlife Sanctuary, 157, 158; Cleveland National Forest, 22; Garland Ranch Regional Park, 101; Guadalupe Nipoma Dunes Preserve, 53, 55; Humboldt Redwoods State Park, 169; Jalama Beach County Park, 63; John F. McInnis County Park, 115; Los Padres National Forest, 35; MacKerricher State Park, 145 ; McArthur Burney Falls Memorial State Park, 155; Modoc National Wildlife Refuge, 154; Montana de Oro State Park, 73; Navarro Redwoods State Park, 142; Palo Alto Baylands Nature Preserve, 108; Parkfield Park, 81; Pescadero Creek County Parks, 109; Pescadero Marsh Natural Preserve, 109; Point Reyes National Seashore, 117, 119; Portola Redwoods State Park, 109; Rancho-Guadalupe County Park, 55; Rockefeller Forest, 169; Russian Gulch State Park, 144; Russian Ridge Open Space Preserves, 109; San Mateo County Memorial Park, 109; Tucker Wildlife Sanctuary, 33; Whiskeytown National Recreation Area, 156
Parks-Janeway Carriage House, 47, 49
Paso Robles, 79, 82
Paso Robles Inn, 82
Pauma Valley, 25
Pescadero, 107; Pescadero Creek County Parks, 109; Pescadero Marsh Natural Preserve, 109; Pescadero Road, 107, 109, 110; Pescadero State Beach, 109
Petrolia, 164, 165
Philo, 141
Phipps Ranch, 109, 111
Pigeon Point Lighthouse, 110

Pine Mountain Summit, 36
Point Lobos, 101
Point Reyes, 117, 119; Point Reyes Light Station, 114, 117; Point Reyes National Seashore, 117, 119
Port San Luis, 72, 73
Portola Redwoods State Park, 109
Purisima Hills, 60
Putah Creek, 137
Quail Lake, 34
Quail Lodge (Resort and Golf Club), 101, 103
Rancho Sisquoc Winery, 45
Rancho-Guadalupe County Park, 55
Red Bluff, 159
Redding, 154
Redway, 164, 167
Restaurant, The, 145, 149
Restaurant 301, 157, 159
Restaurants: Ace in the Hole Pub, 125, 130; Anderson Valley Brewery, 141, 149; Benbow Inn, 167, 169; Bohemian Café, 128, 129, 130; Brass Rail, 167, 169; Cholame's Café, 79; City Café, 89, 92, 95; Deer Lodge, 37, 39; Depot, The, 142; Duarte's Tavern, 109, 111; El Toreo, 33, 39; Hacienda, The, 95; Horn of Zeese, 149; Jonesy's, 142; Julian Grille, 21, 27; Keefer's, 100, 103; Libby's, 141, 149; Los Laureles Lodge, 101, 103; Lucia Lodge, 94, 95; Madonna Inn, 73; Marinus Restaurant, 101, 103; Massimi's Ristorante, 46, 49; Mattei's Tavern, 47, 49; Negri's, 129, 130; North Coast Brewing Company, 145, 149; Parkfield Café, 81; Paso Robles Inn, 82; Quail Lodge (Covey Restaurant), 101, 103; Rendezvous, 145, 149 ; Restaurant, The, 145, 149; Restaurant 301, 157, 159; Station House Café, 117, 119; Taste of Europe, A, 26, 27; Three Points Historic Roadhouse Bar and Grill, 34; Trattoria Palazzio, 39; Union Hotel, 129, 130; V's, 78; Willow Wood Market and Café, 125, 130
Rios Caledonia Adobe, 82
Rockefeller Forest, 169
Routes. *See* State routes.
Russian Gulch State Park, 144
Russian Ridge Open Space Preserves, 109
Russian River, 130, 139
Rutherford Bench, 139

## S-T

Salinas Valley, 100
Salton City, 18
Salton Sea, 18, 26
San Andreas Fault, 34
San Antonio River, 94
San Joaquin Valley, 36, 76
San Juan Capistrano, 30
San Luis Obispo, 72
San Marcos Pass, 48
San Mateo County Memorial Park, 109
San Miguel, 81
San Simeon, 83
Santa Barbara, 48
Santa Barbara Mission, 48, 49
Santa Cruz Mountains, 108
Santa Lucia Mountains, 94
Santa Lucia Range, 83
Santa Margarita, 72
Santa Maria, 43, 45, 55; Santa Maria Inn, 55; Santa Maria River, 55
Santa Rosa, 123
Santa Rosa Creek, 82
Santa Rosa Mountains, 16, 19
Santa Ynez, 47
Santa Ynez Valley, 43, 45, 46
Santa Ysabel School, 20
Sea lions: Albion, 143, 144; Morro Bay, 72
Sespe Condor Sanctuary, 36
Sespe Creek, 36
Sespe Gorge, 36, 37
Shelter Cove, 167, 168
Silverado Mine, The, 149
Silverado Trail, 138
Skunk Point, 152
Skunk Train, 145, 149
Skyline Ridge, 109
Soda Lake, 68, 70
Soda Lake Road, 70, 71, 72
Solvang, 45

South Coast Highway, 27
St. Helena, 137, 138, 139
St. Mary's Church, 116
State routes: Route 9, 110; Route 20, 149; Route 29, 139; Route 33, 36, 39; Route 36, 159; Route 41, 72, 78, 79; Route 46, 79, 81, 82; Route 58, 69, 70, 72, 73; Route 68, 103; Route 76, 21, 25; Route 78, 21, 22; Route 79, 21, 22; Route 89, 155, 156; Route 96, 159; Route 99, 77; Route 111, 26; Route 115, 152; Route 116, 130; Route 128, 134, 139, 140, 143 ; Route 135 (Broadway), 45; Route 137, 78; Route 138, 34; Route 150, 39; Route 154, 45, 46, 47, 51; Route 198, 81; Route 211, 164; Route 255, 158; Route 299, 154–156; Route G15, 100; Route G16, 100; Route N2 (Elizabeth Lake Road), 34; Route S22, 18, 19; Route S3, 21; Route S6, 22; Route S7, 22
Station House Café, 117, 119
Sterling Winery, 139
Stinson Beach, 119
Stratford, 76, 78
Surprise Valley, 152, 154
Taste of Europe, A, 26, 27
Telegraph Ridge, 167
Temblor Range, 70
Ten Commandments Hill, 55
Thermal, 18
Three Points Historic Roadhouse Bar and Grill, 34
Tomales Bay Foods, 117
Tomales Point, 119
Tor House, 101, 103
Trattoria Palazzio, 39
Trinity Alps, 157
Tucker Wildlife Sanctuary, 33
Tulare, 78, 79

## U-Z

Union Hotel, 129, 130
U.S. Abalone, 110
V's, 78
Vandenberg Air Force Base, 63
Warner Mountains, 152, 156
Weaverville, 154, 156
Westport, 145
Whale Gulch School, 169
Whale-watching: Albion, 143, 144; Monterey Bay, 101
Wheeler Gorge, 36
Whiskeytown, 152
Whiskeytown National Recreation Area, 156
Wildflowers: Antelope Valley California Poppy State Reserve, 34, 39; Anza-Borrego, 19, 21; Point Reyes, 117
Wildcat Ridge, 165
Willits, 145
Willow Creek, 159
Willow Wood Market and Café, 125, 130
Wineries: Blackstone Winery, 125, 130; Byron Winery, 45; Cambria Winery, 45; Chateau Julien Winery, 101, 103; Eberle Winery, 79; Foxen Winery, 45; Gallo-Sonoma Vineyards, 140; Iron Horse Ranch and Winery, 125, 130; Mark West Winery, 125, 130; Martin Ray Winery, 125, 130; Meridian Winery, 79; Nichelini Winery, 136, 137, 149; Rancho Sisquoc Winery, 45; Sterling Winery, 139; Zaca Mesa Winery, 45
Winters, 136
Zaca Mesa Winery, 45

# ABOUT THE
# ILLUSTRATOR AND THE AUTHOR

**Earl Thollander** (1922–2001) knew how to live: art, travel, food, music, and writing were all central to his rich life. He was a man intent on slowing down our fast-paced world. A Napa Valley–based painter and illustrator, Thollander spent his early years as a commercial artist and artist/reporter, later turning his attention to his fine art and books. He illustrated thirty-two children's books and twenty cookbooks before he began to write, design, and illustrate his own "Back Roads" books, a series that inspired travelers across the country to discover the tranquil beauty of backcountry routes. Thollander traveled the world to sketch and paint, often leading walking and sketching tours. During his lifetime he earned international recognition for his artistic skill and perception. *Back Roads to the California Coast* is Thollander's last work.

**Herb McGrew** was born, raised, and educated on the East Coast. He was living a relatively normal life practicing psychiatry in Manhattan when, in 1970, his passion for the wines of the world induced him to move to the Napa Valley. He bought an old farm, planted a vineyard, and became a weekend farmer. Along the way he met Earl Thollander and over the years spent considerable time with him—pruning vines, walking through France, and later, as a fan on the delightful tours Thollander led to Mexico, Portugal, Italy, and Malta. In the early '90s, McGrew wrote a series of articles for *Gourmet* magazine, illustrated by Thollander. Thus began the collaboration that eventually led to *Back Roads to the California Coast*. McGrew and his wife no longer grow grapes, but the Napa Valley is most definitely their permanent home.